ANDREW BREWER

Karmic Outlaw
Past Life in The Fast Lane

First edition

ISBN: 9781670910059

This book was professionally typeset on Reedsy.
Find out more at reedsy.com

Contents

III   Rebirth

Dedication

Dedicated to my daughters

Riana Michelle Brewer
+
Lehna Jordann Brewer

Acknowledgements

I want to thank Samantha Whitney, Simone Kross, Angie Ross, Tara Sutphen, Riana Brewer, Teresa Miranda, Valerie Franich, and Debbie Taitel for their incredibly valuable assistance, expertise, and kindness throughout this entire hunt 'n peck past life *process*.

Also a shout out and high five to Scott Grossberg, Nina Barry, Shannon Million, Theresa Byrne, Tom and Trisha Ventker, Megan Lane, Syd Saeed, Shauna Grace, Pam Frasier, Janet Bowerman, Jill Dahne, Suzie Kerr Wright, Aliza Einhorn, Zita Ost, John Koehler, Ronn Jordan, Jane Elizabeth, Stephanie Riseley, Jodie Atkinson, Kris Hyland, Sick Since, Traci Lake Batten, Sarah De La Mer, Julie and Devon White, Sloan Bella, Dai Green, Anais Wolf, Zurab Karumidze, Fiona Aedgar, Jocelyn Alice

Monique Parent, Jamie Clark, Linda West, Karin Katz Sherman, Dina Cox, Joan Atwell, Johnny Sialiano, Sophia Rush, Danielle Egnew, Brian Hunter, Patti Phelan Sinclair, Elisa Lagana, Jan Alexander Seaman, Dr. Linda Salvin, Victoria

Helena Mihatovic, Amy Pierce, Theresa Pierce, Mary Lou Uttermohlen, Sharon Blackstone, Bebe Buell, Mitch Horowitz, Peter Anthony, Coleen Spapperi, Ishtar Howell, Zsuzsanna Budapest, Terri Hulm, Tonya Johnson

and those "on the other side" — my mother and father, Jacqueline + Rudolph Brewer, grandparents Callie + Terry Mainous, Calin Richardson, Lisa Webster, Rosemarie Mincey, Dr. Cindy Brown, Peggy Sue Gerron Rackham (Buddy Holly's "Peggy Sue"), Mrs. Lena Tuttle, the "McIntyre Girls", Roger Brewer, Polly Wolfe Brewer, Ralph + Dee Dee Brewer, Lizzie Saleh, Mrs. Fanny Wilder, Claudia Jennings, Kali DuBois, Ken Harsh, and (most especially) Lehna Jordann Brewer and Stephania Jo Ross

. . . for kindnesses along the way too many to fully list; thank you all . . . your generosity and friendship is truly appreciated, perhaps more than you realize.

I also want to thank my late psychic partner-in-crime Allie Cheslick for years of friendship and advice. I know you're enjoying this !!

A special thank you to Sanaya Roman, for showing me things I could never have learned on my own, the late Mark Strand, Poet Laureate of the United States, for showing me what was possible — how to be a man and creative and magical, all at the same time . . . and, especially, Nikki Giovanni, for showing me love and giving me a model for greatness.

Three brilliant, famous, and incredibly generous people who

touched my life in powerful ways when I needed them most.

Special thanks, too, to the late R. Gary Patterson, "The Fox Mulder of Rock n Roll", for being my pal throughout.

Any textual errors, either factual or grammatical, are my own. I have written this "flat out", as they say, and any and all stylistic "oddities" are also "all on me". I am writer, editor, and designer as a strictly solo act — often a dangerous and, perhaps, foolhardy adventure, yet I have approached this project in just this way. Proceed, therefore, with caution as I am often, in terms of textual adherence to the "rule book", not always one to follow accepted "guidelines" as to what's *acceptable.*

Thank you, too, to Miami University (Oxford, Ohio) for its beautiful campus, fabulous faculty and for providing such a valuable learning *experience* . . . not to mention, allowing me continued access to the university's extensive library system — Knowledge is GOOD !!

Photos of Achille Varzi, Tazio Nuvolari (and Adolf Hitler) are, to the best of my knowledge, all in the public domain.

My profile photos are *Copyright © Trisha Ventker.*

I

Dead Ends

"Currently I'm not a crazy ex-girl friend, but I can't promise I won't be one again"
~ Miranda Lambert

One

Introduction

This is a book about "past lives". It includes theories about how they work, theories about "what it all means", and theories, too, about who I may have been in prior lifetimes. But these are theories and I do not claim to be an expert, not a psychic who "knows all" or a "thought leader" with an irrefutable model and exhaustive supporting documentation. This book is about a *journey*. And journeys often include flat tires and side streets and stale sandwiches and just winging it with no maps, no money, and no umbrella.

Still, when you REALLY want to get somewhere, you will just keep on movin' forward and hope a map shows up later on.

This book is, in part, a lazy day look back at the side roads and the main highways and a little commentary, too, on why I decided side roads, ultimately, were better. I have some trinkets, some treasures, loads of memories, and (hopefully) some new info for the next round of mapmakers.

But this isn't a map; it's a whack travelogue and, as such, you must recognize that not every part of this journey will match the brochure. It's quite possible that we'll take some detours and if detours are not your thing, then riding shotgun with me is not going to be what you hoped for when you booked this trip.

I don't have answers.

But what I do have is a record of how I went *looking* for answers. And if you look long enough, it is likely you'll stumble onto something if not exactly what you'd hoped, at least something memorable and worthwhile.

I have noticed over the years that many of my ideas have rattled some cages and this book is, in some sense (check out the *title*, for God's sake), all about rattling cages. I have written quite a bit over the years about concurrent lifetimes, karmic resonance, biometric matching across lifetimes, Astrological matching across lifetimes, non-locality of consciousness, and "karma" — and my ideas on karma (and probably everything else) are not always in lock step with what seems to be "accepted/acceptable" ideas in the reincarnation "community" (to say the least).

My ideas about every aspect of reincarnation are still/constantly "evolving" as this is not something that can be easily defined or roped off with a cookbook approach listing "all the rules". I wrote a book a few years back called *Cases With Anomalous Dates* (and I am including selected parts of that book in *Karmic Outlaw*) — a book sooooo strange that even I was taken aback. I sat on *Cases* for several years before finally self-publishing it. In the years since releasing it, I have found that many of the concepts first revealed in that book — and even though I don't think of myself necessarily as a medium or channel, this book was most assuredly *channeled* . . . later were "verified" by me in one way or another, including an idea William, the dapper little fellow in the cream colored suit who "spoke to me", first suggested as a past life of my own — a racing driver in the 1920's. This was a new idea to me at the time but once I thought about it, it made so much sense in looking at my own lifetime and in mining the memories and emotional hits I was led to explore this and it was due to William's *suggestion* that after looking in many different multi-colored haystacks, I ultimately discovered a man named Achille Varzi.

And Varzi is Act One in our play . . . Live Fast Die Fast Rinse Repeat.

Put on your helmet, pull up your gloves, strap yourself in . . . Past Life in the Fast Lane. It is time to GO.

Two

Prologue

A champion racing driver, once upon a time quite literally the highest paid athlete in the world, who steals his teammate's wife, destroys his career through an addiction to morphine, and returns, ten years later, to world prominence. One story.

A racing driver so intent on winning that he signs a contract with a German manufacturer before the Second World War, selling his talents, and perhaps soul, to Hitler and the German "machine" who viewed auto racing victories as a chance to prove German technical superiority. Another story.

A third is the rivalry between two men, one a wild child who raced only on instinct, who crashed cars and kept right on driving, even winning a motorcycle race in a full body cast and the other — calm, calculating, precise; technical perfection in a time when technology was far from perfect. You might suspect Driver #1 to be the one to succumb to stolen kisses and the addictive kiss, too, of Morpheus but it was Driver #2, the calm, precise technician, who would see his career crash and burn. But there's another story — and that is a story of rebirth, not of a great champion who vanished from the racing scene only to return years later to prominence, although that story line is evident in his career trajectory.

No, the rebirth of which I speak is literal . . . reincarnation, a famous driver reborn.

Reborn as me.

Karmic Outlaw is, when you boil it all down to its true essence, the story of my quest to understand the things I "saw in my head". I had visions as a toddler, "memories" of another time — but this was the late 1950's and people had no real frame of reference for dealing with a precocious 3 year old talking about fancy uniforms or old cars.

These visions faded when I started kindergarten but began coming back to me, full blown, in my early 20's, not a convenient time to suddenly go crazy.

I've spent 40 quite active years searching for answers as to why I "saw things" and have wandered around the country, multiple times, hanging with psychics and witch doctors of every flavor. Along the way I developed my intuitive skills, too, to a professional level, appearing on national television (including a featured role in a $3.99 a minute psychic infomercial in the 1990's) and being voted multiple times as "One of the Top 50 Psychics in the World".

Achille Varzi in his Alfa Romeo at the 1930 Targa Florio

The driver was Achille Varzi, the 1934 European Driving Champion (equivalent to today's Formula 1 World Champion) and winner of many grand prix races, including the French Grand Prix, Grand Prix of Monaco, the Mille Miglia and Targa Florio.

He drove for Bugatti and was friends with the founder (there is even a Commemorative Bugatti Veyron honoring his legacy, a car that would set you back a couple of million dollars to own), drove for Maserati and was friends with the founder, drove for Alfa Romeo and had a "complicated" relationship with the team leader, Enzo Ferrari. And as a driver for Auto Union, he worked with their chief engineer, Dr. Ferdinand Porsche.

Bugatti, Maserati, Ferrari, and Porsche — Varzi had a close partnership (some harmonious, some not so much) at one time or another with the founders of each of these famous marques.

As a driver, both on two wheels and four, the Batman during these years to his Robin was a man named Tazio Nuvolari, who is still seen by many experts as the greatest racing driver who ever lived — they were friends and rivals and headline news all across Europe in the 1930's. As a "national hero" of Italy, Varzi was under the watchful eye at all times of Mussolini, and as a driver for Auto Union, a team financed directly by Hitler, subject to scrutiny by the German SS. German drivers were expected to join the Nazi Party and some were SS officers. Needless to say, perhaps, but Varzi's time as a driver was "complicated".

Born into a rich Italian family, he was able to buy any car or motorcycle he wished. His success on the track ultimately led to fame and riches and a sponsorship with the leading racing teams of the time. A "playboy" who wore only the best clothes (his racing coveralls were custom made, monogrammed, and always neatly pressed), who stayed only at the finest hotels, a man who was a magnet for beautiful women, his desire to excel perhaps hid a deeper, more complex, psychology.

It is my contention that driving for Hitler and being "used" as a propaganda tool by both Hitler and Mussolini led to his "desire to escape" from Motor Sports and the political machine driving it during the late 1930's.

Varzi had a dangerous job and lived in a dangerous time. The danger in Varzi's life, though, wasn't only on the race track. This story (at least this part of it) is my attempt to understand the connection I feel with this racing driver from long ago; it hasn't been easy nor was it all a straight line from Achille Varzi love at first sight to "yeah I know what it all means and you're it" but I will document (as best I can) my attempts to "come to terms" with what it might suggest about how past lives and reincarnation might work. This book is part bio, part detective story, part how-to manual for searching for your own past lives, part confessional, and part silent prayer.

I have been looking, "seeking" . . . for a long time. This is my attempt to capture some of that journey.

****

The ups and downs of discovering past lives, in a general sense, as well as the specifics of how I came to believe I may have, literally, been this man (and others) in a prior lifetime makes, I hope, sort of an interesting story.

There is also another interesting plot twist to this story. Varzi and I are, quite literally, twins.

Our facial features and body types are practically identical.

10

After compiling my past life profile of who I thought "fit" — initially I looked exclusively for German or German speaking drivers . . . it was more than just a wee bit of a shock to finally discover Achille Varzi, find his story fit almost all of the very specific (and pretty unusual, too) details for which I was searching, and then also see a spitting image of myself staring right back at me!

Me 'n Varzi

There are no absolute answers with reincarnation. As a psychic, if I say something is going to happen, it either happens or it doesn't. There is a means for some level of verification. With past life matches, of course, this isn't true. It is not possible to say definitively this person is the reincarnation of that one; all we can do is look for guidelines and do our best to find people who correspond to what we see, based on speculative models as to how it might actually come to pass.

There is a value, I think, in searching and it is that longing for a "big question" answer that drives my story. This is not a book saying "I am, for sure, Achille Varzi reborn" but, rather, a book saying "I have these memories, I have these impulses, I went looking for some way to explain it and this is what I found — and how I found it!" Please come along and join me on my, literal, ride of a (past) lifetime.

Three

Death Race

They called him the "Black Devil" and like a true demon, he was fast and reckless and, if one's eyes were to be trusted, seemingly unafraid of death. Noted for his wild black hair and his ability to steer his motorbike to victory, while taking crazy chances and (eye test, once more) tempting Fate every time he raced, Omobona Tenni was a crowd favorite, a charismatic wild child, who literally mowed down the hedges with his handlebars racing at the Isle of Man TT, a race he won. The 4 Time Champion of Italy, considered by many the greatest talent in the world on two wheels, Tenni's life came to a sudden and violent end on June 30, 1948 while practicing for the Swiss Moto GP at the Bremgarten Race Track in Bern, Switzerland.

An Italian hero, Omobona Tenni came from a poor peasant family in the Lombardy region of Northern Italy. Always tight for money, he was able to forge a career through sheer pluck. Apprenticed, incredibly, to a motorcycle mechanic as a 9 year old boy, it wasn't until 1931 — when he was 26 years old — that he was able, with the financial assistance of a local motorcycle club, to purchase a Velocette 350.

A true man of the people's champion, Omobona Tenni's death was headline news and all Italy was talking about the death of this great warrior on two wheels.

The national mourning period lasted, though, only about 24 hours, before being eclipsed by news of the death of another, even more famous, Italian champion . . . because on the following day, July 1, one of the greatest racing drivers in the world, a former European Driving Champion, was killed in practice when his Alfa Romeo 158 race car slid on the wet track going 110 mph. That man was Achille Varzi.

When thinking about where to begin this story, I contemplated many different angles. Do I start with my visions as a child and take the story, almost year by year, from my first past life regressions in San Francisco in 1979, through the following years of silent study and hours of guided meditations, on to my early career as a psychic and all the various stops and starts along the way as I tried, not so successfully, either, to figure out "who I was"? That was one angle.

Another would be setting the scene with Varzi in a moment of triumph, a silent film strip of him standing on the podium with the Prince of Monaco after winning the Monaco Grand Prix in 1933 or thinking back to how he won the 1930 Targa Florio with flames shooting off the exhaust pipes of his car as he crossed the finish line. A pretty picture — the "Before Picture".

Or, perhaps, the "After" picture — a great champion, banished from his sport, mind slipping, locked away in a sanitarium trying to shake his addiction? Years lost, his legacy irrevocably tarnished, his "street cred" permanently dented. Where does this story, the story of Varzi and me, really begin?

Ultimately I decided to begin the tale with the deaths of these two Italian Champions in the days leading up to the 1948 Swiss Grand Prix, a race in which Varzi had finished second in his last two appearances . . . the previous year, 1947, when he was beginning his comeback, and the one before that, way back in 1936, as a team driver for Auto Union, just before his career suddenly tanked. Book ends.

So in thinking "where do I start", I decided as good a place as any is to begin my tale with the day Varzi stopped "being Varzi". And so, here we are.

I'd never heard of either of these two men until only a few years ago. Tenni is kind of an afterthought, his part of the film strip only relevant in the oddity of two Italian motoring champions killed on back to back days.

Joined in the mind's eye because of the circumstances of their tragic deaths, one can't help, perhaps, but look at the men side by side, since, at first glance, they shared so many things in common.

Both men were born in Northern Italy, both were Astrological Leos, both former 500cc Italian motorcycle champions, both died suddenly, violently, in their early 40's — Tenni was 42, Varzi 43.

But while Tenni was a poor man who worked and saved, Varzi was born rich and was able to buy any motorcycle or car he wanted — he didn't need a motorcycle club to take up a collection. He wore the finest clothes, stayed at the finest hotels, and was constantly surrounded by the world's most beautiful women. Let's not forget, too, the CARS: Bugatti, Maserati, Alfa Romeo, Horch — exotic, beautiful cars coveted at the time and collected now only by multi-millionaires. A charmed life, but a charm that came, so it would seem, with an expiration date.

Tenni's nickname, "The Black Devil", conjures up visions, perhaps, of demonic nights praying, like Faust, for victory yet it was Varzi, the cool, calculating technician who most likely saw the Devil first hand.

Achille Varzi, Targa Florio, 1930

How does one really fathom a lifetime — perhaps your OWN lifetime in a prior incarnation . . . in which it seems legit to say "saw the Devil first hand" with a straight face? A complicated life and one, perhaps, even more complicated to try to piece together 70 years later, in another body, with a new name and new identity, in an entirely different set of circumstances. But after 40 years of "hard driving" looking for an "answer", this is what keeps showing up: an Italian racing driver who threw it all away — who later put it all back together, only to see it destroyed in an instant on a wet Summer day in Switzerland in 1948.

Varzi's career was filled with twists and turns and sudden crashes, but almost all of these were crashes *off* the track; Varzi was a very precise and careful driver who had only two major wrecks in his entire career, one driving for Auto Union while high on morphine and the other, one of his only mistakes behind the wheel (we won't count the ones while not in the car), leading to his almost instant death when his car flipped over after hitting a curb.

His life is often seen by those looking back at him as a case of what might have been, a great champion who fell asleep at the wheel of his career at his personal peak; that's the story most often repeated (although I think there is more to it than just that) — a man addicted to morphine, chased from the sport in which he excelled. His story is a ride not just fit for a Grand Prix Champion but also the famous Mister Toad, whose storybook ride was wild, indeed.

****

The Circuit Bremgarten opened in 1931 as a track for motor-cycle racing; the first auto race was held there in 1934. A track with no long straightaways, Bremgarten was a series of high speed corners and seen as a very dangerous place in which to race — this at a time in which modern safety concerns were of no concern at all, so dangerous then would likely be seen as total madness today. Following the tragedy at *The 24 Hours of LeMans* in 1955, in which 83 spectators were killed and another 180 injured, racing was banned in Switzerland and the track is no longer used. Irony, perhaps, that the last race here was held in August, 1954 when I was just a little sperm starting to take shape within my mother's womb.

When you look up information about this track, one thing that always stands out is the idea that the track, because of the uneven quality of the surface and the trees overhanging the circuit, was especially dangerous when wet. Is this an afterthought, since many drivers (Varzi among them) were killed here on wet surfaces, or was this common knowledge straight from jump?

Knowing nothing about the track, other than the fact that Varzi died here, I decided to do some research — I'm writing a book, you know . . . and discovered that one of the other super famous racers of the 1930's, Rudolf Caracciola, crashed here 4 years later, ending his career, his leg shattered, in 1952. In 1948, days after Tenni and Varzi were killed, another driver, Christian Kautz, a young, talented racer from Switzerland and son of a multi-millionaire, died during the race after crashing his Maserati at high speed on Lap Two, killing him instantly. Three drivers killed in just five days.

And they all were killed in pretty much the exact same spot.

There is a private memorial to Varzi now at Bremgarten; it has a photo of Varzi above his name and a couple of paragraphs about him. A large silver cross is beneath the photo and a small wreath in the upper right corner of his picture. All of these items are nailed into a tree, a makeshift tribute to his legacy. The curve where they all died is now known as "Tenni Curve" and, to my knowledge, the Varzi memorial is the only one visible along the circuit, even though numerous drivers were killed racing there.

I watched a few videos on youtube trying to get a feel for

what the track was like. I could see, pretty quickly, that this must have been a hair raising experience driving at speed with filled potholes everywhere and overhanging trees shadowing the track, as well as raised curbs along the pavement just waiting to throw a car or break an axle. But the main feeling I took away from these videos was one of peace — it was a beautiful place, with (to me) kind of a magical vibe. I felt strangely, and surprisingly, serene.

Perhaps a good thing to see on your way out; all these beautiful trees, driving a car super fast and sensing nature all around you. Not such a bad place to go, I thought, and so a new layer of weirdness was added to my world — trying to "remember" dying at Bremgarten.

Four

Black Sheep Squadron

I have written quite a bit about reincarnation. I have talked about my theories on past life matching (I believe there will always be a strong physical match between you and each other lifetime in addition to a strong Astrological synastry between you and all your past lives, too) as well as my theories of non-locality of consciousness and why I think we reincarnate in the first place !!

All of these things I will get into, again, here in this book. In looking back at some of my past writings, collected on my website www.andrew-brewer.com, the very FIRST blog I found (or did it *find me*?) was one from January, 2017 called *speed bumps* . . . this seemed sort of synchronistic to me so I am including it here:

****

19

most challenges in life are (really) just opportunities to examine what works and what doesn't

looked at in this way, nothing really stops you, although like speed bumps on a city street, they may slow you down a bit and annoy you

but (also like these same speed bumps) these annoyances serve a valuable purpose in helping you focus on how best to move forward with the fewest risks, if you allow it

everything can be changed . . . once you understand

. . . that everything can be changed

change your mindset and your future changes too

#truth

****

You may be asking: why include a short blog about never giving up other than the obvious weirdness about speed bumps?

I think past lives all connect, but not necessarily one after another in a "straight line" manifest destiny kind of way (more on this later). We can see them thematically grouped together in "clusters" of interlinking lifetimes, rather than strictly as stand-alones; translated, I believe we have a group of lifetimes that somehow interact with one another and as we come to some level of consciousness in one, we add to the consciousness of the collective.

To make a whacky idea sound even whackier — as we change this life in 2019 (and we change it because we see it with fresh eyeballs), we also change another life (or two, or more) from 1937 or 1832 or whenever. Seen in this way, perhaps Varzi's crash at the Swiss Grand Prix is a healing opportunity for me 70 plus years later as I begin to understand (or at least TRY to understand) how he and I might be "one and the same". The curb that killed Varzi at Bremgarten is also a healing salve for me years after the fact as I begin falling in love with the process of dying and "returning" and all the magic these linked "experience clusters" gift me.

Seeing the continuity between Varzi's experiences and my interpretation of my own — *interpretation* being the key word here . . . allows me to appreciate the beauty and symmetry of LIFE and, in seeing this divine beauty, allows me, also, to see that divine beauty within me.

This is important.

As we come to see value and magic within ourselves, the quality of our life improves. This is not rocket science nor necessarily an earth-shattering insight. But the added bonus of seeing your life improve through finding continuity in past life experiences that are BLENDING with your own may, perhaps, shine a light on living that is not so readily apparent.

The question you may be asking perhaps sounds something like this: "how, exactly, am I supposed to find who I was? And, even if I did find them, how do I then isolate the experiences THEY had that are blending with my own?"

To answer that question, I have to take a short side trip and look at some of the most common ideas about "karma" — and why my vision of how it works is so different than what most people seem to believe.

I don't look at karma in the eye for an eye, tooth for a tooth kind of way that many seem to think must exist — I shot you in 1745, you've come back to shoot me today. I don't think we come to work off "debts". I believe we come, instead, to "express our truth".

Many people see reincarnation and karma as a step by step progression. We keep coming back, seeking perfection (a word I don't like, by the way) or atoning for past sins (a concept I disagree with — and also one I believe short circuits people's ability to stand in their own power) in hopes of getting to the "promised land", a Heavenly reward based on our good deeds accumulated over a series of lifetimes.

We've been bad, so we keep coming back trying to get better. Yet we're bad by nature, so we have to suffer and suffer and suffer some more, to make up for the "fact" that we've just been so bad !!

I think this is nonsense. I don't think there is any *truth* to this, at all. In fact, I believe the concepts of a malevolent God or a never ending series of karmic debts misses a very important point . . . which is? I think we come because we've created something incredible and we want to keep coming back in order to show it off again and again and again.

So the answer to the question "how, exactly, am I supposed to find who I was? And, even if I did find them, how do I then isolate the experiences THEY had that are blending with my own?" is simply this: we find our past lives by finding what we love.

And we find what we love by finding out (best we can) who's trying to convince us that's not what we *should* love. That is the first brick on the Yellow Brick Road to discovering your past life.

What do you love — and who told you that loving this was a bad plan?

That is how you find your past life.

I think we start off having it goin' on straight from the get-go and our journey(s) on Earth is more art project than after school detention. I think others try to confuse us about spirituality and reincarnation more than help us when they talk about karma as a price you pay. It's not.

My trip, this round, down (past life) memory lane is an attempt to speak up for those who've felt there was more to it than just one and done but couldn't find information that resonated with how they "felt". I came to express my truth that I love it here (although some days are better than others hahahahahaha) and I want you to feel that same way.

Feelings MATTER !!

The essence of who we are (think of this as "the soul") and who we were (think of this as your individual incarnations) are both revealed by who and what we LOVE.

Which leads me to another topic: past life regressions and spontaneous past life memories.

Past life "regressions" are now the "Gold standard" for recovering "past life memories". I (personally) do NOT think this is true . . . (to me) "karmic resonance" (unconscious but persistent "affinities") are the key to recognizing past lives.

Find what you love within yourself, discover what themes (places, music, food, styles) light up your soul, and get quiet and allow those themes to wash over you. Memories are great but the energetic flash one gets when one sees something familiar is, in my opinion, more important.

I use those flashes of "affinities" as the guide for discovering past life themes and, from there, continue to drill down deeper and deeper to possible real life matches. But, whether one finds a match or not is nowhere near as important as the discovery of what you love — because armed with this information, you become virtually unstoppable.

As a psychic I can sometimes end up "sharing" the brains and memories of a lot of different people; does this mean was I "them"? Of course not. But I have come up with imagery both through regression work and clairvoyant imaging that corresponds to fairly obscure but historically verifiable data about people and lifetimes that, for sure, "weren't me". This doesn't happen all the time, of course, but it DOES HAPPEN.

Memories are not how I find past lives — I look for emotional triggers or, put another way, do I continue to have "reactions" to things I see or read about? These reactions are the catalyst for me to drill down more and more until I start peeling the past life onion. Is this a slower, more roundabout way or getting there? Yes, of course.

Would it be more efficient to just remember names and dates and places? Absolutely !!

But most of us, as adults, don't have these memories nor can they be fully trusted, if perchance we do, as unique to us and not a blend of old movies and fantasy thrown together willy-nilly. There has to be a *continuity* to past lives. The past life has to *connect* to the ones that come later. There has to be something that passes on from one go-round to the next to the next to the next. What is consistent in them all?

More importantly, what does this consistent theme tell us about who we are?

Going back to my earlier statement — "The essence of who we are and who we *were* are both revealed by who and what we LOVE" . . . in knowing who we ARE, we can't help but begin (if we choose to approach our lives in this way) building a model of what might have caused this unique ME to develop. Childhood, of course.

DNA, of course. Early education, classmates, coaches, "heroes" — all valid building blocks imprinting themselves upon us.

But not everyone in the family, (with the same parents, comparable educations, similar DNA structures), comes out the same. Some "wild cards" show up who march to different beats.

That group — The Black Sheep Squadron . . . is filled with people struggling to find who they are and what they love, because they've been denied legitimate access to following their dreams. They're taught that their dreams don't matter, either because they're "bad dreams" or because the person dreaming them doesn't deserve to have this dream come true — they're not good enough, tall enough, pretty enough, smart enough, rich enough, enough enough enough. Enough already.

Too many of us are taught the dream life, the one that matches the essence of who we are, is not legit for us to repeat. And so we take side roads trying to find a substitute to get there and after enough detours and flat tires and two dollar 7-11 hot dogs you just give up.

Give up, give in, and simply go forward on any road you can find, no more maps, no more itinerary, only just surviving on the highway, looking for a place to sleep and another two dollar hot dog and maybe, hopefully, a pleasant encounter with another stranger along your journey, someone equally as lost and frustrated as you.

Black Sheep are the outliers, the ones who don't completely accept what's "been taught". They are also the most likely people to find their past lives utilizing the methods I will share with you throughout the rest of this book.

But before we do that, let's go back to Achille Varzi and the racing world of the 1930's — a time when technology and sport each took a giant growth spurt and where one of the world's top drivers took a very definite step . . . backwards.

Five

Motorsport is Dangerous

*Achille Varzi in his Alfa Romeo 6C 1750 Super Sport, Targa Florio,
1929*

Kate Walker, in her piece about Achille Varzi on crash.net, begins with this classic opening, so delicious I am including it here as a lead in to Chapter 5: *"Motorsport is dangerous. It says so on the tickets, and proof can be found in the history books. But while motor-racing is a dangerous occupation, so too are women and morphine, as pre-war Italian legend Achille Varzi discovered to his chagrin."*

It says a lot about not only Varzi's life but Varzi's legacy — and the illicit nature of affairs and drugs in how others frame the story and structure of one's life . . . sex, drugs, rock 'n roll, fast cars, pretty corpses. Varzi, the calm precise ruthless champion driven to win is now full on punk rock.

Steal your wife right in front of your nose and fuck her in the bathroom while you wait outside, drive race cars flat out after shooting up morphine, skip races, give a big "fuck you" to Hitler and Mussolini and just throw money in the toilet because you're in love and now an addict and "living in the moment" . . . that's some outlaw shit, right there . . . right?

Self-destructive? Unlucky? Cursed? Or seeking "rebirth" through dying and wanting to come back from the scrap heap? Who knows, for sure, what went on in his world. I don't and can never fully know as my relationship to Achille Varzi is through "emotional resonance" and so I am not able to have full recollection of the events of his life.

Does this mean I wasn't him? In my opinion, it does not. I had memories, impulses, "pictures in my head", that later I was able to match to events in Varzi's life and with the other elements present in his story and physicality, build a hypothetical case that he matches what I'm looking for and is a likely candidate to be "who I was" in a prior lifetime.

What are some known facts of Achille Varzi's life that I can use as a starting point to find out a little more about "who he was"?

Achille was born on August 8, 1904 in Galliate, Italy, a municipality in the Piedmont region of Northern Italy, about 25 miles west of Milan. This is critically important information as it gives me his birth date and, with that, a chance to do his Astrology to see how well it might match my own. More on this in a later book !!

Varzi's family were wealthy textile manufacturers. He was the third son of Menotti Varzi and his wife Pina Colli Lanzi Varzi. His uncle, Ercole Varzi, was a cofounder, along with his father and Paolo Rossari, of the Rossari and Varzi Manufacturing Company, as well as being a Senator and Fascist politician.

Varzi's older brothers, Angioletto and Anacleto, raced motorcycles and Achille started racing himself and was doing quite well by the time he was 17 years old, in 1921. He quickly began beating his older brothers and was Champion of Italy at age 19.

After a few championship seasons on two wheels, Varzi moved on to racing cars and, just as he did on motorcycles, started winning races and making a name. He was not afraid, though, to jump ship from one manufacturer to another, even if that meant driving a car that wasn't made in Italy — not a positive PR move, by the way. This happened when he began driving for Bugatti (France) in 1931 and later, in 1935, with Auto Union (Germany).

Varzi won many races and was always a competitive driver. The great German champion, Rudolf Caracciola, said of him "When you saw Varzi behind, you shivered". And Enzo Ferrari, a man with whom Varzi had a somewhat complicated relationship, said "His style reflected his personality: intelligent, calculated, ferocious in making the most of his opponents' weaknesses. I'd say he was ruthless."

Known as something of a man of mystery, he was seen by many people as cold and aloof. Juxtaposed against his friend and rival, Tazio Nuvolari (who was outgoing and straightforward), the complexity of his character was drawn in even greater relief than might have happened were it not for the constant comparisons between the two. Personalities sell newspapers and in the 1930's each man was worth quite a few inches of print each week.

After a successful year racing in 1934 — he won the European Driving Championship, Varzi could see that the new machines coming out of Germany were the cars of the future and if he was to remain competitive moving forward, it was imperative that he drive for a German team.

Auto Union (a combination of four manufacturers who merged together, as a result of slumping sales arising from the 1929 "Great Depression") and Mercedes each were funded with 250,000 Reichsmarks each year, money spent on developing engines and chassis that would prove to be unbeatable for the next five years.

Varzi signed a contract with Auto Union for the 1935 racing season and all seemed well. He was at the height of his powers as a driver and seemed destined for even greater things. But, as often happens in life, what appears to be a blessing is, in actuality, a test. And part of the test questions revolved around a strikingly beautiful young blonde by the name of Ilse Pietsch.

Ilse was the 22 year old wife of a reserve driver for Auto Union, Paul Pietsch, who later became a successful magazine publisher and lived to be 100 years old. Ilse was soon with Varzi and well stealing your teammate's wife — especially if she's German and he's German and you're not and you work in Germany and are financed by Germans promoting the Master Race etc etc etc . . . was probably not a "career-enhancing" move.

Ilse entering the story seems to be the pivot point where — forgive the pun . . . the wheels start to fall off. Because Varzi was in love, crazy in love. And Ilse was the one who introduced him to morphine. And morphine and racing cars are just not the best companions.

And so, slowly and then quickly, the tides turn. And therein another tale doth lie.

It is also (the morphine addiction, that is) THE most critical piece of why I believe I was Achille Varzi. That, and the Silver Arrows (the sleek silver racing cars produced in Germany during the 1930's) were the two wild cards in my search — and I was skeptical, even though it was what I "saw", such a driver existed. But Varzi had both — the Silver Arrows and the addiction and once I found this, I became more and more convinced I'd found my match.

Throwing your career into turmoil for illicit love — yeah, I had that same experience this round, too. An addictive personality? Yeah, I have that, as well . . . only not (this round) with drugs.

The morphine and the fact that he drove for Germany helped seal the deal for me that Varzi and I might be one and the same.

The fact that we're twins certainly doesn't hurt either !!

And the twin part is the focus of my next chapter. Because, in my opinion, every past life looks a LOT like all the ones before. Lord knows, Achille Varzi and I do, indeed, look very much the same.

Six

Biometrics

I am certainly not the first person to put forward the theory that past lives look alike. One theory involves the concept of biometric matching. Dr. Adrian Finkelstein talks about this in his book *Marilyn Monroe Returns: The Healing of a Soul*. In this book, Dr. Finkelstein shares his work with Canadian singer Sherrie Lea Laird, who had memories that she came to believe suggested she may have been Marilyn Monroe in a previous lifetime. There can be little doubt that Sherrie and Marilyn look alike !! In exploring the idea that Sherrie's physical commonalities with the late actress enhanced the likelihood that she was Marilyn reborn (an idea I share, too, by the way), Dr. Finkelstein mentions the Facial Geometry Matching work of the late Dr. Paul Von Ward.

Dr. Von Ward talked about this idea quite a bit in his books, especially *The Soul Genome*. In *Soul Journeys: Past Lives and Reincarnation (2011, 2013)*, author Rosemary Ellen Guiley recalls an interview with Dr. Ward in which he stated that "data I've collected in the Reincarnation Experiment suggests that each of us inherits a psychophysical legacy from a unrelated deceased individual". He suggests, too, that this legacy "appears to shape biometric factors such as facial geometry, ear forms, body types, hand and finger proportions, and hair patterns".

each of us in our 20's; Me on the left, Achille Varzi on the right

Dr. Von Ward identified several characteristics from biometric science that he considered most genetically stable. These were: (as mentioned above) body type, facial geometry, ear form, hand and finger shapes . . . as well as voice and odor. Odor is not one I can use, of course, and voice is not something easily discovered, either (at least in most cases), but, like Dr. Von Ward, I also use body type, facial geometry, ear form, and hand and finger shape as important measuring sticks when comparing two people for a possible past life *match*.

I also use body movement, too, in those instances in which film evidence is present that would afford one the opportunity to make such a comparison. In the few film strips I've seen of Achille Varzi, it appears that his facial movements, hand gestures, and manner of walking are all markedly similar (actually *eerily* similar) to my own.

There are many different schools of thought when it comes to the legitimacy of biometric markers in reincarnation. Many past life researchers dismiss this idea out of hand as unlikely. Past life researchers also, in most cases, seem to take a dim view of psychics . . . and I've tangled, hard core, with quite a few reincarnation *gate keepers* over the years who felt that my job title disqualified me from voicing an *informed* opinion. Let's just say we often "saw things differently".

Their desire to apply rigorous methodological controls to their investigation is admirable yet to discount all non-traditional means of "data retrieval" — like *clairvoyance* (when there is no defined data source from which to draw information in the first place) . . . seems (to me) incredibly short-sighted.

Suggesting (for example) that birth marks (perhaps reflective of a prior life wound) are scientific and biometric analysis of photos is not seems incredibly close-minded and not all that scientific — at least to me, as there are no controlled experiments one might use to test this hypothesis, either direction.

I persist in my theory that biometric commonalities will be present in all "valid" past life matches — translated: you will always kind of look the same, every time out.

You may be a different gender, different race, fat one time, skinny the next, perfect porcelain skin or the exact opposite, all these variations will be present . . . but the basic blueprint and basic facial *structure* (in my opinion) will always look sorta the same.

Seven

The Magical Apprentice

When thinking about a title for my last book, I ultimately decided to go with *Cases With Anomalous Dates* — a title, by the way, most people didn't seem to like.

"Cases with anomalous dates" was a term first introduced by Dr. Ian Stevenson, the distinguished Professor of Psychiatry at the University of Virginia whose work on reincarnation paved the way for so many of us to follow.

Dr. Stevenson studied over 2,600 cases of children who had "past life memories" and who provided evidence of dates, places, friends, and family members of their "prior" lifetimes.

But in several of the cases studied, Dr. Stevenson found that the current incarnation "began" before the prior incarnation "ended" . . . Dr. Stevenson said, in referring to these situations, that they were "cases with anomalous dates of death and birth".

"In a small number of cases [from Dr. Stevenson's files], the subject was born before the person whose life he remembered died. (The intervals vary between a day or two and several years.)

"In a case of this kind, taken at face value, it would seem that the subject's body was fully made and presumably occupied by one personality before another one took it over.

"The quickest way to rid oneself of such awkward cases is to suppose that errors have been made in recording the dates, and in some cases vagueness about the exact dates supports this conclusion.

"I have satisfied myself, however, that in a least ten cases of this type we have obtained accurate dates and the anomaly remains." — *Children Who Remember Previous Lives, (1987) by Dr. Ian Stevenson.*

Dr. Stevenson speculated that these cases may not, actually, have been instances of reincarnation but rather, "body theft or possession". In my book, I looked at the idea that these "cases with anomalous dates" weren't instances of possession but rather the actual "mechanism" by which a small group of souls chose to experience life.

The *irony*, perhaps, is that the large parts of that book were inspired by a "voice", (whether that be considered a piece of the subconscious, or a disincarnate "entity", or a ghost, or a nightmare, or any number of possibilities), "inside my head" who, in various ways, "dictated" large parts of the contents. Was I, myself, *possessed* by something (or somebody) trying to make me believe, erroneously, that concurrent past lives are possible — who knows? Truthfully, who knows.

I don't nor can I ever . . . but I lean very much in the camp that believes what I saw was not an "evil spirit" but, rather, a messenger from God. However, you say potato I say orangutang . . . no one can ever 100% fully *know*.

This voice is, to me at least, connected to an image, one I have "seen" for close to 40 years — a dapper little gentleman in a cream-colored suit, with spats . He always reminded me of the late novelist Tom Wolfe . . . who goes by the name of "William".

Of course in spending so much time working with past lives it is pretty much a given that, by default, I have also spent quite a bit of time thinking about death.

It is kind of an interesting subject.

And, in thinking about Death, I've also spent quite a bit of time thinking about an afterlife and/or ghosts — things not fully dead that somehow "show up". As a result of that, I was able to "hang" with William (and the others "I've seen" over the years, as well) and accept that whether it was all madness or not, there was a *continuity* to the madness and this continuity was ultimately my launching point to say "ok, dude, show me what ya got".

Really, in order to understand life, understand the hows and whys, understand what's under the hood driving the car down the incarnation highway, I think it is kind of important to take a peek (in whatever ways possible) behind the curtains of the *Great Beyond*. As a clairvoyant and "remote viewer", I spend a big part of my day trying to see things in the "future", so why not point the lens towards what happens after we pass?

In fact, I do meditations many times where I slip into such a deep space, sliding away from breathing, shutting the motor down, slowing the pulse, slowing it all . . . down . . . and thus, as a result, I am, quite literally, pushing myself through the walls "between", sort of a re-birthing in reverse.

It is not for the meek or faint-hearted. It is, quite literally, a "trip" but 40 years of intense meditation has given me some of the best tools possible for making this journey. In order to "jump" between life and death, I have to push the envelope quite a bit — it is the only way I have been able to slide into this space where I can, for instance, describe places as a remote viewer while driving home in rush hour traffic on the highway.

My mind has this "picture in a picture" thing that I doubt many people have — but I do. I bring all this up to give you some idea as to how I have come to believe what I am about to tell you.

I believe, very strongly, that there is a divine essence — call her God, Goddess, Nature, Pure Energy, Cosmos . . . whatever name rolls off the lips — that permeates everything. We can see this, in a modest way, in the whacky world of quantum physics but we are but simple creatures stumbling along in the palace with only a match and a short stick.

I also believe that (somewhere) there is a world that looks like ours, that feels (in some rather remarkable ways) like ours, where our soul essence (a small holographic slice of the totality of the divine essence) stops and "sits for a spell" in that in-between breath between one mortal coil and the next . . . 'cause I believe, too, VERY STRONGLY, that we slip into a new suit of clothes in the same way, pretty much, that we step into a new life, wrapping the skin and bones and muscles around us, with that new car smell, off to new adventures, new movies in the mind, that we can replay lounging around the world of the Spirit later on.

That's what it is, ya know . . . a chance to take pictures to play over again in the divine world of the spirit — a game, but a game with a purpose, a chance to smell and taste and love with all our might, to rev the senses UP, to belly up to the smorgasbord of experience, to sample the beauty of love, of sex, of magical levels of accomplishment, tempered with drastic bungee jumps of the spirit into states of despair, loss, a wild roller coaster ride but one amusement park passes into another, a century passes, a new life begins, and ends, and begins again.

There is no end — death is a recall, a chance to trade the old Buick in for a new Lamborghini, or an '82 Yugo — depending on one's needs and from that standpoint I make my choices, "buys me ticket" . . . knowing, as I do (in the ways in which one can possibly, truly know anything) that I will circle round this way once more and all my past triumphs, all my past failures, are but a day in the life . . . a chance to experience something magical.

Believing that life is magical is a choice, an attitude. It is the attitude I take towards this wild ferris wheel of ups and downs and to the extent that one can ever really enjoy one's time, I try hard to live fully awake, with no fears.

Not that I am totally fearless; of course, that's not true. But, still, many of the things that pass for supreme importance in the day to day tick tock world don't matter to me in quite the same way as, perhaps, they do others. I can walk into the light of past lifetimes, castles, pretty girls, nights that were magical in some particularly magical way.

I see this not only for myself but for others, too. For example, in this particular lifetime, I know my "car" has some super fancy extras and I don't want to trade it in just yet. My turbo is rockn and I want to ride on down the road a few more miles before I turn off the key for the last time.

But my jolts into death's realm, languidly rolling in the wild berries of her wisdom, has shown me that there is no fear "there", rather a beautiful respite and soon, from that magical world, the itch will once more need scratched and then my soul will fly through space/time into a new little body and the ride, once more, will magically begin.

****

In my published work, I have talked quite a bit over the years about "remote viewing" and non-locality of consciousness. There is, I believe, a force, yet undefined, that serves as the "bridge" yet it is not REALLY a bridge, in the literal sense, as things are working in multiple places all at once.

This, perhaps, seems contradictory to what our senses can "sense" but I am quite certain it exists, nonetheless. On top of that, I believe our "soul" essence also works within this "level of multiplicity" so that we can be impacted by events at a distance (because those events evoke emotions, and it is the emotion that serves as the jet fuel for "transmission") as well as be "associated" with multiple bodies, all at the "same time".

Reincarnation then may ultimately come down to something akin to the "oversoul" that runs multiple bodies who are pieces/parts of a specific "spiritual core".

We are fragments seeking unity — reincarnation, how it works and what lessons it holds, is a key component, I believe, in "figuring it all out".

****

I haven't talked a lot about my "apprenticeship" as a psychic. For one thing, the stories are almost tooooo bizarre to be believable and, in spite of all I've said over the years, there is a strong component of my personality that gravitates towards fairly rigorous logic and analysis . . . and a fairly conservative bent towards my position in the "public eye" — which of course I have repeatedly shattered but such is the basis of one's psychology :)

In April, 1979, I went to San Francisco, in theory to work / slash / train as an actor / slash / model but my actual career lasted probably about 8 minutes and even the few times when I talked my way into something, I always (and who knows why) blew them off — or simply forgot to show up.

As an aside, I find it incredibly ironic that in 1979 I went to California to be an actor and ended up as a psychic and in 2009 I went back to California to work as a psychic and ended up working as an actor :)

In San Francisco, I took a class on Past Life Regressions in July, 1979 and met a woman at the class named Adella Pickering, who taught classes herself on past life regression, who was sitting in on this class, since our instructor had previously taken a class with her. I "volunteered" to be the guinea pig and did a regression in front of the entire class — I had never done, nor seen, nor even imagined, anything like this ever before . . . and in my regression I was a King, in Germany, in what I took to be a small kingdom, kind of like the equivalent of being the King of Butler County.

I am pretty fluent in European History now, but in 1979 not so much. Luckily, there was a woman in the class from Austria who confirmed the historical accuracy of what I was describing (in the 18th Century there were dozens of small kingdoms scattered throughout what was then The Holy Roman Empire) and she suggested it sounded a lot like Southern Germany . . . earlier, I had visited a psychic (one who specialized in "past lives") at a giant psychic fair at the old Cow Palace in San Francisco who, after meeting me, literally, just shook his head and told me "you've got a tough one."

Not what you typically look forward to hearing when you visit a psychic !!

I initially asked him: "I have this weird thing about Victorian houses. The furniture, the buildings, I have dreams about them — they seem 'significant' to me, somehow. Is it possible I had a lifetime where I lived in one of these houses?"

He said to me "In your Victorian era life, you were a woman.

46

And your husband tried hard to please you, but you gave him a bit of a hard time." I remember him talking about a "sexual" something but honestly I was in kind of a daze and don't really remember.

Then he said this:

"You've been a King, many times. And that is why this life will be hard for you. But you've already been a King; it is not for you to do that this time around." For those who know me, or think of me as the Psychic Diva, you may be thinking I asked him to tell me this hahahahaa . . . but when I was 24 it was the LAST thing I would have ever thought of and if I wanted a possible past life scenario, it would have been this: "you led a very nice comfortable life and lived in a nice big comfortable house and starting this time next week you will once again be doing the exact same thing."

But that is not what he said.

I was kind of in that awe-struck what the fuck did you just say kind of space and asked him how he did this ?? He said "well, you can do it, too" — and I assured him there was no way in the world I could do what he was doing . . . but he insisted — and then his wife started talking to me once I left and said the same thing "oh you'll be doing what we do."

I went home that night after the first class and did the regressions myself. We'd done them twice during class so I had a fair recollection of the steps. Relax first, then the journey up the mountain, walk along the side count 1 to 25 step by step see the mountain picture it in your head. At the top, the guide . . . then another count and finally the doorway. Step through it, back into the past, back into a life "relevant to the life you're living now."

Reincarnation. Was it really possible?

For months after that, I did them every day, kept the days and trips in a notebook, page after page after page. At first, I was a doctor, a pediatrician it looked like, living in Baltimore, born 1903 died young in a fire in a big beautiful Victorian home with a wrap-around cream-colored porch. Then I was a composer, studying at the Prague Conservatory with Dvorak, who, I later discovered was there during the years he/I studied there, 1890-1893. A doctor and a classical composer . . .

I had my validation, a historical "hit" — Dvorak at Prague. I had been playing (let me *correct* this, I hit keys, sort of) the piano for the past year; so being a composer made sense to me. I was convinced. A verifiable fact; it was true!

But the lives started piling up. More and more and more lives — all lived in the 1900's. It wasn't possible to be all of them. What did it mean?

And then things morphed again . . . I won this little toy tiger at Pier 39 in San Francisco playing "whack-a-mole". Actually, won two of them and in our apartment on Dwight Way in Berkeley there was a little hook hanging from the ceiling, so one of the tigers found a home there. At first I didn't pay much attention to it but after a while I noticed that when I looked at the tiger it would "rotate". The tiger's arms were held up so the paws were both parallel to the head, like a mini goal post.

Each time I would look at the tiger, it would move. OK . . . a few days of this passed and then I started putting my arms into the same configuration as the toy tiger and when I looked at it, I held my arms like the tiger's and rotated at the hips. The tiger seemed to like this and moved more. Within about a week it became pretty obvious that there was something "unusual" going on.

Fast forward again — shortly after the first class, partly

due to my new found status in our band of merry souls as a reincarnated King, and probably more due to my then current state as a fairly good-looking 24 year-old guy, I started talking to Adella and got her phone number and was invited to her birthday party in Marin County.

It was there, in the kitchen, that I met a woman who I didn't pay too much attention to — since I was focusing more on this incredible dark-haired exotic recently divorced beauty from Malibu who "flew up for the party" and who told me that if I came down to see her she would let me drive her Rolls Royce . . . anyway, for some reason SHE seemed to capture my attention and the woman in the kitchen — she said her name was "Sandy Roman" — did not register with me in quite the same way.

But there was someone at the party I did want to meet. She was a specialist in past lives and had recently written two fairly well-received books on the subject, *Reliving Past Lives* and *Life Before Life*. Her name was Dr. Helen Wambach and she was a good friend of Adella's. The big topic on everyone's lips that day was not past lives though — although my reincarnation experience as a German King was already well known before I arrived — but instead something I'd never heard of before called EST, with a dude named Werner Erhard. A lot of the people there were big in to EST and tried to convince me I needed to go . . . however, I was a poor boy hanging out with millionaires and so our world, and experiences, were gonna be different.

Any of you who may be familiar with the old book, and movie, *The Serial*, will have a fairly good idea of how my afternoon went.

My "psychic abilities", latent for 24 years, were now EX-

PLODING . . . I talked to Adella a couple of times and she promised to hook me up with this person and that person and somebody else — but she finally said "I will get you in with Sandy. She's the most amazing psychic I've ever seen. She knows all about you and has offered to help you."

****

So, that is the high-level, super-abridged history of how I ended up in Sanaya Roman's Oakland home one Saturday afternoon in the Fall of 1979.

There are psychics and there are good psychics and there are REALLY good psychics — and then there is Sanaya Roman. I think I'm "pretty good" but nobody's like her . . .

So much happened that day. I was there for a long time; I'm not sure exactly how long, probably 2 or 3 hours — and I wasn't there for a psychic reading, although that was part of what happened. The reason I was there was to try and harness this VERY tele-kinetic power, a highly electrical power, that was literally ooozing out of my pores. In 1979 and early 1980 when I looked at something . . . it MOVED. Never did it before and have never been able to do it since. However, for about 4 or 5 months I was literally able to move things, tele-kinetically — which is fine when you want to . . . confusing, but fine.

It is not so fine when THEY move, whether you want them to or not. Such was the case with the young neophyte on her doorstep — a prodigy coming to the Master for guidance. I was, literally, on fire and I needed help to control it. Enter one Sandy Roman.

Fast forward once again . . . I did quite a few different exercises with Sanaya. It was she who taught me how to use my "third eye" by pushing light out of my forehead and many of the exercises I use in my classes today, I learned that afternoon with her. I am not going to talk too much about that but instead want to talk about what I "saw" that afternoon when I was "under".

****

In my session, I connected to what might be referred to as discarnate entities or something akin to an out of body hello here is your higher self looking back at ya . . . I was given many pictures of the future and especially my place in the future at some soon to be arrived at destination still light years ahead.

I was told for the first time that I was a reincarnated Confederate Army officer from the American Civil War and another theme that was new to me came up, as well — one that has been a constant ever since — a VERY strong past life connection to Eastern Europe.

I was also told there were "lines across the earth" and when the lines "criss-crossed, there it is a sacred space" . . . at this point I had never heard of "ley lines" or anything even remotely close to this — so this bit of information was new, and fairly significant in that it did not correspond to anything I'd ever heard of, yet I was later able to verify the possibility of what it might be.

There were a lot of things that happened that day — and I am not going to go into all of them but . . . there are two things I want to talk about that came up in this session.

One: the idea that matter was changeable. Sanaya went into the session with me and was seeing what I was seeing. She talked about a time when I was a high priest in a civilization that used mind control and what we would call magick long before recorded history. She said that I was one of the MOST advanced practitioners and that ultimately I would re-discover the secrets of how matter was transformed.

What I saw was this: you took a fluid that you found in a fish, you put it in a tube and then you used it, sort of like a "magic wand", to literally "transform" matter. The tube was a fluorescent green and it was kind of like the glow sticks you see at clubs when everyone is E'd out . . . I also saw myself flying but the way I did that was like a corkscrew . . . very tight turns that allowed me to levitate. Is this true?

Is it madness?

I honestly don't know. But it is what I saw — and it is what SHE saw.

I was "told" this civilization was called "The Luodovicians" . . . I have never been able to confirm anything about an ancient civilization with this name but incredibly the theory of a magic fluid found in a fish I did find in the work of Carl Jung . . . it is called a remora, or "sucker fish".

Second concept: I was given a very clear picture of the earth's magnetic field "shifting" and the lines criss-crossing the earth coming more and more into play in the days ahead. I believe the time is coming when this magnetic "shift" will soon occur.

This session with Sanaya changed the course of my life and ultimately led me to follow a path that challenged me in countless ways. It was due to what I saw, and experienced, in 1979 that I followed the "path" that laid the groundwork that underscores the foundation for this book.

****

Ultimately, Reincarnation is about LOVE . . . and as we move from time zone to time zone, bopping in and out and in again

. . . finding challenges galore

still we keep coming back in order to feel, and experience, LOVE — in all its many beautiful colors, with one leg up or one leg down

not everyone is attuned to the "past life beat"; that is sad, but understandable

but just as the dog responds to the whistle you cannot hear, your ability (or inability) to "remember" doesn't change the dynamics of birth and rebirth

there is a purpose to this life, and all lives, and as we move along the karmic foot path we stumble along sometimes blindly, sometimes not

seeking the beloved

there is love and there is the one who loves back . . . God is the ultimate lover and no matter how much hatred or destruction or disarray, that love is the driving force for all that we do

reincarnation is, in my opinion, the key to EVERYTHING and as we move along, seeking and sharing love, through all its many ups downs and in-betweens, we come back — over and over and over again . . . to feel that faint echo

from loves that we shared and walks that we walked — this is why we return

to find LOVE once more

it doesn't have to be romantic love, sexual attraction or anything of that nature. if it is, wonderful . . . if not, it doesn't really matter

everything is about "returning", a homecoming — a reunion with the self and with the "other"

finding and sharing love in all its many flavors, each time with different backdrops, different songs

but, ultimately, still the same

II

Lane Change

*"If you're under control, you're not trying hard
enough."*
~ Parnelli Jones

Eight

"The William Material" Part I

Throughout most of the 1980's, I was back living in Ohio and marginally "attending classes" at The Ohio State University in Columbus (primarily so I could use their Rec Center and their Library). In the fall of '87, I moved into an apartment off campus that was a couple of blocks from a 7-11 and since moving boxes and furniture makes me thirsty, I took a break and walked up the street to get a giant guzzler of Diet Pepsi and, on the way, walked past a little shop I'd never seen before filled with books. A bookstore to me is like a bakery to a sugar addict and so, God and circumstances were (once more) conspiring to change my world.

It is this little bookstore, called *Pearls of Wisdom*, that set the scene for "the changing", although certainly I didn't know any of that at the time. Inside this magical little store were books and crystals and all sorts of things I hadn't seen since my pilgrimage to San Francisco eight years earlier.

And sitting at the front of the store, behind a glass case filled with stones and wands and delicacies galore, were four super model women talking about Astrology.

My desire to show off to a pretty girl, in this case 4 pretty girls, accidentally led to my professional career as a psychic. T'is true. After wandering around the store for about 15 minutes, glancing back at them, seeing them all glancing back at me, I finally blurted out "I know a little about Astrology".

And so, with these words, my professional career began. I talked to them about Astrology for a long time, read their charts for them and after I was done was asked, no begged, to do a live event for them coming up in a few weeks as a grand opening for their store.

I was petrified to do this and might never have done it (or anything else) had the owner not insisted. I said no, she kept asking, I said I'm not sure, she said you'll do great and little by little I gave in, not because I wanted to do this event — because, for sure, I DID NOT.

I did it because it give me a chance to hang out with this woman and hanging out with her listening to her tell me how talented I was and how much she wanted me there seemed like a good idea. Cupid's Arrow was banging on my heart; not such a convenient thing as we were both married . . . and not to each other. Cupid, though, his fucks given quotient is zero and well, stuff happens sometimes.

Within six months, I would be working at this store, be the resident morning psychic on the biggest rock station in Columbus, and have clients galore; I would also no longer be married, either. I was soon kind of a mini-celebrity on the "Psychic Scene", I guess you could say, and as the cherry on top of the rutilated quartz wand was given the nickname "The

Psychic Adonis". Things weren't so bad in my world in 1988 !!

Looking back all these years later, the two years at *Pearls of Wisdom* were probably the happiest ones of my life. But my bullheadedness would soon inspire me to toss all this in the trash.

Some times in your life are slow and steady and not much seems to happen. Other periods are forest fires and 24 hour a day INTENSITY. The old epitaph on the dead gunslinger's tombstone — "well he packed a lot of hard living into his short but eventful life", that was the readout flashing on the radar gun.

But all that is another story.

This next part of the story, though, is about chaneling. And channelers. And my very first "paid gig" in metaphysics: being a body guard for Mafu.

****

No doubt you're saying to yourself (most of you anyway) "what exactly is a Mafu?"

Mafu is/was an *entity* channeled by a young woman, at least young when I met her, named Penny Torres. Penny was a California housewife who somehow ended up as the vehicle though which Mafu (a 32,000 year old *being* who had incarnated on Earth 17 times) "spoke". I liked Penny. She was lively and pretty and had funky little cowboy boots and well, sure, I was happy to guard her door to ensure no one would touch her robe without paying the requisite toll first. That toll, back in 1987, for a 3 day weekend seminar, held in The Sheraton downtown, was $150. Money I didn't have, nor would it have been something I'd have done anyway if, on the off chance, I had a surplus.

But my "new friend" thought I needed to have the Mafu *experience* so she arranged for my work study stipend as the body guard so I could attend, for free.

Back in the 1980's, channelers were kind of a "thang". There were channeled books everywhere: Ramtha, Lazaris, and many others. And channelers with books were also likely going to be channelers who offered live seminars.

Mafu was part of this wave and many people hung on her every word. Is she legit? Who knows. Are any of them legit? Who knows — although I met Sanaya Roman and I'm here to say that Sanaya was AMAZING and so, for sure, she gets my vote as being the real thing.

As to Penny Torres, I liked her, I found the three days "interesting" and I was glad I went. But I am not what you would call a *fan* of channelers or channeling , not before Mafu nor certainly after.

But fan or not, the following 4 chapters were, without a doubt, *channeled*. And I was the one doing "the channeling".

A funky little dude with bleached out hair in a cream colored suit, wearing spats. Not only did I channel him, I also saw him. Lots.

Is he legit? Am I insane? I have no idea, at all, as to the *truth* of either question.

But legit or not, crazy or not, here we go . . . I give you "The William Material".

****

What is it that reincarnates: The soul is like a three-headed toad. Each mind connects to one heart, one set of limbs, but one head looks to the left, one to the right, and one straight ahead. When a spirit animates a body, each of the three directions may join together in one physical space. Or — conversely — one may choose to look left or right or straight down the middle and to accommodate each way of seeing, a body and a full set of fingers and toes created.

In other words, one may choose to experience the right or left hand path on their own, without benefit of the "middle mind". These are the souls who walk to a different beat and, as such, they are quite literally split from the original Soul Creation.

When a soul entity chooses to walk a left or right hand path, the driving force of the spirit manifests as a holographic "slice" of the entity. Each piece of the soul still exists, but the thinking/feeling mode is partitioned, so that one can best and most easily slip into a set of circumstances commensurate with the path they are choosing to live.

If one splits, then one takes the risk of tipping. Such are the dynamics of what Dr. Stevenson refers to as "cases with anomalous dates". You are an example; you lead six lives at one time . . . three to the left and three to the right; you never choose to be in the center. This is "unusual" but not impossible. This is typically done to connect with the widest range of experience; this is the profile of a "thrill seeker" but often times these individuals lead lives of "quiet desperation" or, other times, lives of intense activity and high personal achievement. This profile is one in which the greatest rewards are possible, but the greatest risks are undertaken.

How does one choose what life to lead: There are spiritual "counselors" who work with the incarnating spirit, aligning with the time place and sets of circumstances most likely to bring about the types of experiences one is seeking. Incarnation is primarily a tool in which one grows through "experience" and the evolutionary journey of the soul is accomplished in the Spirit Plane; it is not fully realized as a living entity.

Each experience is brought back and through the analysis of the "intersection between experience and emotion", the soul is able to see how best to reach a state of "silver light". Silver light is the spiritual equivalent of a Baccalaureate degree. Gold light is the spiritual Ph.D.

But the experiences are only fully embraced in the "light world". The shadows of a physical existence are too great for a full, honest and non-judgmental approach to seeing oneself in the full-length cosmic mirror and so that is how, and where, souls "evolve". It is done after the life is lived, not during.

For you, your spirit path is one of extremes; the left path typified by a life as a German Military Attache in the 1930's or a racing car driver in the 1920's; the right hand path typified by your life as the Russian poet, killed in the War, or so many lifetimes as a monk or spiritual acolyte. In this life, you are leading the Right Hand Path, but you have chosen to allow the left hand path to "bleed" into your consciousness. As such, you are a Right Primary, with a Secondary Left. This often is the path of a schizophrenic or a Holy Man. It is not the path of one "steeped in tradition".

However, you are a traditionalist, in the classic sense, and so this life, as opposed to most, is one in which your natural instincts are turned on their head. Normally, you would choose a Left Path with a Secondary Right — the path of a Leader, a Spiritual Warrior but in this incarnation you have flipped that and, as a result, are too often at war with yourself

The William Material Part I

and your "ideas", attitudes that are grounded in a different time and place.

In those lifetimes in which you have chosen the "Right Path" you often have focused on being a "light bearer" and have sublimated the Left — this is more the profile of a spiritual teacher or artist. Often times one sees the same personality manifest in these different "roles", so the choice of being an "artist" or "spiritual teacher" is largely based on fundamental aspects of the culture in which the entity chooses to incarnate.

Choosing to allow these darker, more aggressive energies to blend with your artistic, spiritual "side" adds a bit of turbulence, but a life in which these extremes are brought into harmony is one in which, to adhere to a concept often used, large "doses of karma" can be "burned away". Not exactly a lifetime of penance, still there is an element of self-abrogation to the harmonics underscoring this incarnation and the life circumstances as delineated in the native horoscope.

Why would someone choose to reincarnate as a Left / Right "Split": Remember, the "goal" of the Earthly incarnation, as a purely spiritual exercise, is to understand one's self within the context of one's physical and emotional "response patterns". In order to best conform to the old dictum "circumstances reveal character", someone might choose to do this in order to maximize the number and type of experiences they would encounter, in order to more fully, due to having more "data", determine "who they are" more quickly, or they might choose to take on additional "tests" so as to achieve a better "balance" on the "Spiritual Plane" — due to their increased breadth and depth of self-awareness.

The ultimate goal of all lives, then — when looked at from a spiritual perspective, is to learn about one's self in order to ascend to the various "levels of existence" within the Spiritual Plane.

This concept seems strange to many but, in essence, it works like this. There is a spiritual hierarchy, much as there is a pecking order within institutions and groups on Earth. Souls are working through multiple steps along the way as they move into higher and higher spiritual realms. The concept of a malevolent or unforgiving God is a human construct. That is simply not the case. One is not judged by the level of spiritual attainment in the "Light World" . . . everyone can ascend and time is fluid in a way not easily understood within a 3 Dimensional Earthbound model.

All souls work at their own self-determined pace to achieve whatever level they wish to achieve. There is no judgment, at least not in the manner in which you may see it on Earth. There are levels of awareness but there is no sense of lesser/greater. All is within a state of harmonics on the Spiritual Plane.

Choosing a life of relative sameness is often the mark of a less "advanced" soul – as they do not wish to overwhelm themselves with too much data to analyze after their time on Earth "ends". Those who take on multiple trials often are souls wishing to learn quickly; even if the situations are less than ideal, the response one has to the "trial" is instructive. Those trials and tribulations on the Earth plane are the core reasons one chooses to have a "complicated" life. Movie stars and others with extreme ups and downs are souls that "can take it" and so they have chosen to accelerate their learning by increasing the types of experiences they will take back with them.

There is black/white in all lives. Those with big swings, though, are normally souls with higher aspirations for spiritual advancement. Think of it as a "pay me now or pay me later" type of decision. Choosing to pay the price on Earth helps accelerate the level of understanding, and (as a result) the speed with which one advances, on the Spiritual Plane.

Where do we come from originally: All creatures of Pure Light are aspects of the divine Godhead. Think of it like this — a piece of the Godhead is infused in every soul being. This piece, like an atom on Earth, is a seed from which the soul manifests. Another way to think of the Godhead is to think of the Godhead as if the Godhead was a tree. Soul pods grow, much as an apple grows on Earth. Seeds from the fruit are the basis for the individual souls who will later choose to incarnate on Earth in order to further their spiritual and psychological growth.

You could look at life on Earth, in one sense (and a very meaningful metaphor it would be), as fertilizer for the soul. The soul grows because of the properties inherent within the push/pull, up/down nature of Life on Earth and the cumulative weight of these lifetimes on Earth assists the soul to grow bigger and stronger. Without the Earth's influence on the soul/seed, the individual would not reach his or her full, Divinely written, potential.

Taking the metaphor a step further, the apples — or what I refer to as the soul pods, are comparable to what some on Earth have postulated as an Oversoul. Yet, the Oversoul as a concept is a faulty one, as it typically is taken to mean that individual souls all connect to a bigger "thing", much like an Organizational Chart in a Corporation in which all the employees under a specific Manager are all part of a distinct and separate team. It doesn't work that way.

The Oversoul is not distinct from the individual soul, nor

67

does the individual soul fit underneath it, as a child might fit under his mother's umbrella. All is connected, since each seed was grown originally from a sprout of the divine Godhead's breath. But the Oversoul is primarily a means of transmission.

As the soul/seed develops, various incarnations are explored in order to assist the soul/seed in bringing forth its most beautiful flowering. The flowering of the soul/seed is done in the Light World, but the growth is done on the Earth. One cannot bloom without the Earth's fertilizer, yet the blooms are not revealed except in the Spiritual Plane.

Spirits, then, who will make the fully conscious choice to split, so that they might soak up the nutrients of the Earth more quickly, do so with the understanding that there is a very great risk involved in doing it "this way". If a plant, for example, has its branches cut away, so that the cuttings might grow into another separate plant, there is a minimal risk to the original plant but a much greater risk to the piece "cut from the original" as that piece must have the proper conditions in which to grow and is more fragile due to the fact that the cutting does not start from a "seed"; however, the chance of seeing multiple healthy plants is often seen as being worth the risk. So, too, is the thinking behind souls "splitting".

As we mentioned, souls who split must go through the Right Mind or the Left Mind. They cannot stay in the Middle Mind and, as a result, a part of their "total package" is voluntarily abandoned. Those who split must, at a minimum, be advanced enough as spirits so that they are able to survive with much of their legacy left behind. It is not a prospect for a weak entity nor one without a fairly adventurous nature.

How do people actually "split": The choice to split is made in conjunction with Spiritual Counselors on the Spiritual

Plane; it is through looking at the available time frames and individual horoscope/destiny filters that a soul makes the choice to incarnate — and when. The circumstances are not fully within the free range of the incarnating spirit as basic cosmic doctrinal laws, based on astro-genetic themes, must be followed.

However, within a fairly narrow range of choices, the basic soul blueprint can be established and the entry points defined and accepted. Astro-genetics, the integration of astrology and Human DNA, is an intricate dance that is formally decided upon before each incarnation. There are generational and regional backgrounds through which the soul must travel. It is impossible to customize the environment. However, one can build a myriad of fine points to the psyche that will intersect with the communal energy in order to "jump start" the variants that are unique to an individual in his or her pursuit of a bank of experiences and "reaction opportunities".

Many people talk of soul contracts. The idea of a "soul contract" is actually not true, at least not in the sense in which most people typically envision it, although the concept and terminology is grounded in a greater truth. Certain opportunities exist within the astro-genetic formula and fulfilling certain agreed upon tasks is part and parcel of the earthly "experience".

Each entity is under his or her free will to make choices to respond to situations and provocations as he or she sees fit. However, regardless of the desire for an entity to feel as if they are capable of making conscious choices 100% of the time, the dictates of the cosmic destiny wheel are fixed and, as a result, the choices open to the entity on the Earth plane are not limitless. Patterns are set early on and generational momentum swings the pendulum one way or another, so the concept of "free will", as most people see it, is also erroneous. The only totally free choice an individual has is his or her emotional response; but even that is filtered, to a large degree, by unconscious thought patterns that are instilled in the child through family and/or cultural dictates which are far beyond the control of the child to alter.

No entity, no matter how evolved, is fully in control of their emotional response pattern. However, these cognitive frameworks are completely understood when one sets about to review his or her life in the Light World after the sojourn on Earth has ended.

When a soul splits, the choice is made with the full recognition that these generational and cultural forces will impact the range of emotional options available to an incarnating spirit. That is a given. Where it gets a bit more complex is in the fact that, since the "Middle Mind" is closed to an incarnating spirit who chooses to make the split, it is often difficult for that spirit to find a balanced approach to life.

They are, by nature then, somewhat extreme in their choices and response patterns. This is one of the problems that all souls who split will face and for many it is reason enough not to attempt it.

Nine

"The William Material" Part II

How does someone recognize they are a "split" incarnation: This is a difficult question to answer as most people will not be privy to this recognition. There are many reasons for that — the primary one being, of course, that it is often contrary to the soul's purpose of acquiring additional information about one's self through an additional incarnation if too much time and energy is spent looking at other lifetimes, lifetimes which would already be looked at on the Spiritual Plane during the soul's prior interludes in the Light World.

Not everyone is well served by being allowed to see other lifetimes. Again, this is a function of the spiritual needs of the incarnating spirit and is not contingent on "spiritual advancement" nor is it a reward from past incarnations. Having this bleed-through is a decision made in the Light World and, as such, it comes with huge risks to the incarnating spirit as too much focus on past glories will blind an individual to the current state.

Why, then, do I, personally, have this knowledge: The reason you are open to past life influences is that, to a large degree, you are attempting to turn a past life "upside down" . . . in other words, you are saying, spiritually, "OK, perhaps I blew that one. Give me another chance and I will try again."

This is more common than you might think. Many people will "regret" past choices and wish, in essence, for a second chance but remember — the only second chance available is the opportunity to test one's self in a "comparable" manner in a later incarnation. There is no opportunity to reverse a choice and the attendant action made within a specific lifetime.

But, for those who wish to see what might happen if put in a similar situation a second time, taking into consideration any cultural and genetic differences that must go along with a new incarnation, in many of these cases a glimpse into the past is given, but it is given in the spirit of a "wake-up call" or warning. OK, last time I did this, so this time I better keep a close watch so I don't do that again.

If you are shown the how and why of a past life, more often than not, it is the result of something the individual soul is seeing as a "mistake". But, like all things associated with split incarnations or split levels of consciousness, the desire to advance must be strong enough so that the individual spirit accepts the "noise" these visions bring and is also willing to incorporate them, in some meaningful way, in to his or her "current" lifetime. Choices, therefore, are made through the prism of past experiences in a way that is both unusual and a bit complex, as well, relative to the cognitive processes of "most" people.

You, personally, have "abused" power in the past and, therefore, are being tasked with making choices in this current lifetime in which you put the needs of the spirit ahead of any short-term needs for ego gratification or whims of your personal, which at times have been quite ruthless, ambition. Your competitive nature has been "short-circuited" in this lifetime, too — in order to more easily give you the space necessary in order to see why these attitudes from the past won't fully serve you as someone who is seeking spiritual advancement in your current incarnation.

This is a "tough one" — but it is a necessary exercise as you work your way towards a more balanced and spiritually integrated whole. Not everyone is willing to do this, but I don't want to make it out that this is all a bad thing. Some choices work better than others. At times, an incarnation may be undertaken with the express purpose of re-adjusting the personal thermostat. That, in a nutshell, is what is happening with you.

Ten

"The William Material" Part III

Why would a soul choose to suffer: One of the reasons people "choose to suffer" is because the feelings associated with suffering — primarily a heightened state of arousal — often compel individuals to display a response pattern that is both unusual and extreme. As a result, the alteration in consciousness brought about through intense states of anxiety or grief tilt our response mechanisms in such a way that we have an entirely different "bank" of data with which to work after we pass back to the Light World.

As a result, suffering is a gift, although it is not one, certainly, that most enjoy. But, the modification of the internal stimulus-response model precipitated by intense emotional swings provides valuable lessons for an individual — both on the Earth Plane as well as the Spiritual Plane later on. Suffering is a vehicle for rapid progress and those who choose long-term, seemingly chronic, pain and suffering (whether this be physical or emotional is not important) are being gifted with a change in consciousness that is absolutely unique.

Also, due to the transitory nature of most emotional pain, at least pain which is brought about through a "crisis", this state of being (and the response patterns undertaken within the midst of traumatic periods) allows an individual to experiment with various modes of behavior that, although entirely unique to a given situation, are still fully grounded in the types of attitudes unique to that person.

It is a laboratory, in one sense, in which various modes of being can be explored. Ideally, one grows through self-awareness but regardless of the time frame in which an individual reaches heightened states of being in his or her Earthly lifetime, the changes brought about due to trauma allow for an individual's rapid growth in ways not easily replicated in times of peace or full mental, and emotional, clarity.

How does one shift from being "in emotional pain" towards a state of being that is more "emotionally balanced": This shift in consciousness is one that can only come about when an individual decides that the feelings associated with a new way of seeing and doing outweigh the benefits associated with maintaining a state that is familiar.

People often fall into chronic patterns in which they feel as if their life is not "working" — this is not the same as a life of suffering. Far from it.

This is actually a life of comfort . . . the comfort being one in which the restrictive element associated with limited expectations allows the individual to more easily escape the responsibility of choice — and thus minimize sudden changes in emotional state, resulting (of course) in an escape, as well, from the pain associated with huge variances occurring within (and to) the emotional body.

I realize this goes against much of what you might think; why would pain and suffering be a blessing and how is it possible a life in which so many dreams are unrealized might actually be a choice, made by an incarnating spirit, to have a "simple life" as opposed to someone who took many risks and was able, through whatever means necessary, to make substantive changes in their lives, through their own efforts? Still, it is the "relative" sameness of the lifetime that most closely corresponds with the spiritual aspirations of the individual spirit. A spirit that "splits" almost always leads a lifetime in which wide swings occur throughout the course of the individual's life.

Remember, split souls do so with the express purpose of maximizing the number and type of experiences possible for them within the shortest window of time. If one were to look towards a life of slow, incremental gain they would not take upon the burdens associated with splitting. As a result, it is often a large part of the split soul profile that these spirits suffer quite freely — yet, invariably, they rise above, at some point, any restrictions that are placed upon them only, perhaps, to later dip back into a state of loss and anxiety, in order to test themselves as to their resiliency and recuperative powers as they work, once more, towards a more elevated and integrated personal space.

Split souls, therefore, often lead lives in which much happens — but not all of it, necessarily, "good" nor easy.

The choice to incarnate as either a left or right split, therefore, is undertaken with the caveat that large "swings" are likely within the individual lifetime. It is the combination of a personality type actively seeking, and pre-disposed, to adventure and the limitation imposed upon the incarnating spirit that many of his/her strengths must be abandoned "before coming" that add to the probability of a life filled with high degrees of variance. Split souls are often psychologically vulnerable and, as one might imagine, drawn to artistic or entrepreneurial careers.

A life of quiet consistency is not the typical profile associated with a split soul.

Eleven

"The William Material" Part IV

Is there a way to integrate a split soul while physically in the body: The integration of a split soul is the ultimate goal of an individual . . . the typical way in which this may manifest comes about through a recognition that the spiritual core is "elsewhere" and by making conscious decisions to honor that spiritual "home", it is possible to "re-integrate" the left and right.

This can only come about through direct experience of the God force, what others term "gnosis" and even that is not enough; one must catapult one's self from the physical body into the etheric body.

How is it possible to move from the physical body to the etheric body: The movement from physical to etheric happens through a transformation of consciousness, based on expanding the frames of reference to which one normally adheres. There is consciousness and then there is heightened consciousness.

The integration of thought with sensory awareness is the bedrock foundation for this shift in 'cognitive state". Think of it like this: many people, especially in Western cultures, are defined, cognitively, by language. The words they use, the concepts associated with those words, and the style and syntax in which those words are used to form "thoughts" all underscore the pathways for understanding.

In essence, the map DOES become the territory.

Those who "split" do so with the express desire to test themselves. They do this with the understanding, prior to incarnation, that there is an expectation that they may "fail" but the rewards associated with the chosen lifetimes are so great that the incarnating spirit accepts that risk.

As we spoke of earlier, the desire of the incarnating spirit is to "test" oneself in order to fully reveal character. It is this "test/revelation cycle" that underscores the basis for choosing to incarnate on the Earth. Without this, most would choose to stay in the Light Plane.

and it is here that
the "William Material"
ends

Twelve

Red Pill Blue Pill

All this stuff with William happened eight or nine years ago . . . initially, I was kind of dumbfounded as to what it was and, for sure, what to do with/about it.

Six lives at a time, right hand path, left hand path, etc etc etc. Wt fuck ??

Varzi showed up after William. Most of the potential "matches" about whom I now feel most confident have all "shown up" post-William. Something in how I went about looking for them changed. And as how I looked for them changed, so (too) did I.

I have postulated several different versions over the past ten years as to how concurrent lifetimes might work. Initially, I came up with something I called the "Stick Figure Theory of Reincarnation" in which I postulated binary splits that could split into a secondary binary split, as well. Translated into English, I thought that if you "split", you incarnated in three tracks, not two.

This binary splitting theory was an outgrowth of trying to force William's "six at a time" pronouncement into a formula that could apply to more than just me. Subsequently, I have rejected this theory, at least certain parts of it . . . of course everything I say about reincarnation is *theoretical* and I am not afraid to say it is all a work in progress, so I might change all this tomorrow. The primary thrust of this book is not "hey look at me, I've got it all figured out" but, rather, this confused the fuck out of me when I was a young man and here is how I went about trying to alleviate some of that confusion. And I am still trying.

There are several models in which the ideas *presented by William* might make more sense — the primary one, perhaps, being the concept of a *monad*. In that scenario, each lifetime would connect to the others through something much like what is typically imagined as an oversoul. One means for drawing this up might be to look at the oversoul as being the "soul father" and the individual incarnations the children. It could also be possible that, oversoul or no oversoul, I (somehow) live in 5 or 6 bodies simultaneously !!!

I think, though, it more likely that if we split, we split into two or three "lanes" only, not six. However, this is my psychic detective brain at work here and so the truthful end of the day answer is "who really knows — or *could* know?". But the *ideas* from the *William Material* were foundation pieces as to how I went about building models for how it all might work.

So, where am I at, right now?

First off, I *believe* we ALL reincarnate. Everybody.

Yes, I know YOU are the exception and there's never been another one just like you, never was, never will be. Even so, I believe every single person alive has reincarnated . . . some more than others and some perhaps two (or even three — or 6 or maybe even more; again who knows) at a time.

But, far as I can tell, *everyone* reincarnates.

****

I have revised my "Stick Figure Theory of Reincarnation" to the following. I believe people fall within 4 primary buckets.

One group, probably about 95 % of all people, goes one right after another, nothing more nothing less and I have that group broken down into "themes" that deal (in a simplistic form, with some variations) with chakra "drivers". They also are likely to take some time between incarnations. This is not a group that necessarily likes change and they (in my theory, anyway) will stop for a bit before jumping back into a new body and a new "set of downs".

Translation: people will fall into basic "types" and those types will continue to roll on, lifetime after lifetime. You don't change your spots although you will, quite often, move to a different jungle in order to see how you will "adapt" to a different set of circumstances. But the basic building blocks of your personality will come back, over and over and over again.

You come back to "express your truth", every time. And your truth is relatively consistent every time out . . . we are tasked, each lifetime, with walking in integrity, treating others (as well as ourselves) with respect and dignity, finding some source of inner power in order to more effectively navigate through each lifetime.

```
We DO NOT, however, come back totally different than
before -- we will look and act much the same each
"go round" . . . circumstances will influence us,
social mores and family "rules" will certainly be
undercurrents to what we do -- and how "we do it",
but the nature of who we are, the essence of who we
are, is (to some degree) fixed . . . I realize this
will upset many reincarnation purists but that is
how I see it.

We come to express our essence, to express our
singular truth . . . each and every time; each time,
too, we will share certain qualities with all the
lifetimes before (and yet to come).
```

There is a flamboyant, competitive, rule breaker in every one of my lifetimes, a golden child Beau Brummell "talker" concerned with Beauty and less so with "practicalities" . . . a flake perhaps but one with style and also one, in spite of what's on the surface, with a laser beam intellect to go along with it — it is "who I am", even with the lifetimes on a horse, with a sword, the flamboyant rule breaker is never all that far beneath the surface.

And so, too, with you. What makes you unique and magical you bring with you, every time.

Your basic blueprint will roll on, in different flavors but never without many of the same basic core ingredients. We come to share our essence, we come because we like it here, we come because it is the best place to hang our Art and be seen.

We are *consistent* in our uniqueness. We come to express truth, not to find it — to *express it*. That is what we . . . do.

****

The next group I call the 1 + 1's . . . basically, one "with a trailer". This group goes fast and furious and may actually overlap one another by — my "guess" . . . up to around 2 or 3 years, either direction.

Then there are splits and lastly, *binary* splits . . . where the splits "split". The binary split folks are much like the 1 + 1's: risk takers who *like to be seen* and who thrive on *lots* of change. They are high energy peeps who will be drawn, quite often, to lifestyles in which they are able to "do their thing" unimpeded by rules or restrictions. The binary splits and 1 + 1's are drawn, too, like moths to a flame to vocations in which they have lots of variety and also opportunities for lots of attention . . . Entertainment and Politics are vocations tailor made for this *type*.

In looking back at *The William Material* and attempting to frame "splits" and "binary splits" into dominant styles, I think it likely that "splits" always tend to reincarnate on the "same Left/Right side" while binary splits tend to jump around a lot. A perhaps overly simplistic way of describing a complex idea, but that is how, now, I "see it". Binary splits go fast and furious and wear many hats, while "plain ole splits" often have a highly developed skill they keep repeating over and over — and the split is more akin to the old man in Lane One is fading out as the new one in Lane Two goes through school and begins his/her development. This group *may come* because what "they bring" . . . we, on Earth, *need*.

Me, mid-50's . . . what's my "type" ??

Each group breakdown will share similar "styles". In my *theory* it is possible two (or more) people, living all at the very same time, "are connected" to the very same soul essence, even if their birth and death dates overlap. They would have to have VERY tight astrology with one another, because this (to me) is the final frontier as well as lots of other similarities, including physical — think DNA . . . you can tell he's a Brewer even though he doesn't look exactly like any of the others; still, that Brewer "something" is "visible".

In the following section I will expand on this and a lot more and talk in much greater depth about how I think it *all works* — Chapters 13 through 17 include pieces I've written in the past and so will bop around a bit from topic to topic. In Chapters 18, 19, and 20 we will look, again, at Achille Varzi and how his life and mine may be seen, perhaps, to mirror one another.

We will also take a peak under Destiny's fig leaf to examine what that possible mirroring effect might mean for me (and perhaps, you, too) as we be-bop together down the Cosmic Highway.

And so, on we go, to **Section III: Rebirth**.

III

Rebirth

"It took me a long, long time to learn what I now
know, and I don't want that to die with me."
~ Frank Sinatra

"Let's play two!"
~ Ernie Banks

Thirteen

Quoting Myself

Achille Varzi at the 1932 Tunis Grand Prix

Each child comes in to this life with an "optimal path" — the highest integration of all the various talents and desires one has, all lined up and moving towards an expression of pure and total Love

This "optimal path" is based upon his or her genetics and past life "themes".

Then we lead whatever lives we lead. The difference is a fairly straight forward mathematical formula:

"where we are" minus "what our optimal path should be" equals

"our karma"

****

You have a "karmic familiarity" with certain types of people places and/or situations

The fish out of water thing many of us may feel is due, in large part

To the dissonance between your "core essence" and your current "space" . . . But your soul seeks what "it knows" and when you find "your space" you will suddenly "feel at home" . . . This is why it's possible to change your life situation in a heartbeat

Because when you're home

Shit works

To quote myself "who you are is where you end up"

****

Sometimes people may assume if they are having "issues" with someone this is a byproduct of something labeled (erroneously, I believe) as "karmic debt"

in English, this person is a goofwad and makes my life HELL, so I must have burnt them alive in the 12th Century

I don't think that "assumption" is necessarily always true — or ever true

because implicit within that idea is the assumption of an "eye for an eye" causal relationship between past "actions" and current "re-actions"

when the truth is more likely that the situation in which you may find yourself is not grounded in "karmic debt" but instead really an opportunity for growth that is "hidden" within adversity

you don't "owe" something as much as you have "contracted" for a certain "type" of experience . . . by seeing adversity or conflict in this way, it is easier to "accept the lesson" and grow and, also, "move on" we learn when we learn and not a moment before . . . everything in the "physical world" is an opportunity for growth and a chance to see ourselves through new eyeballs — the true "purpose", I believe, of our earthly journey

****

 . . . *"exceptional people tend to reincarnate as exceptional people"*

I believe there is a driving force within some people to find a "higher" level of achievement — even if that is never "actualized" in the 3D world and they fail to meet with "success"

I also believe that some people start off as "different" from the others; in my opinion, they, literally, have an extra gear

and so, as a result, they are "driven" in ways others maybe are not . . . also, it is common (as I "see" past life "themes") for people to have more than one "vocational calling"

for example, my primary "job" in the past has been, as far as I can see, a high ranking Army officer . . . yet I also have many lifetimes in which I was a monk, spiritual teacher, etc

plus the artist wild child lifetimes, just to add some spice

it is not unusual, to me, to see people who are fairly well-known and to imagine they have been "well-known" before, even if that was for something way way different than what they are known for today

As I "look" at people in understanding their past life "profile", I see them "show up" to me in terms of what I have called "thematic buckets"

think of these as being analogous to vocational groups — some people's "evolution" is worked out through a backdrop of the job/"calling"

while others tend to see their spiritual evolution best facilitated through interpersonal "relationships"

ultimately, our spiritual "progress" is measured by changes "within" and those changes are ALWAYS a result of interactions, (and our responses), with other people

we cannot grow without others — even if we live in a cave, all alone, it is our understanding of our self in relationship to the greater big bad universe

that serves as the yardstick for our own internal "quest for harmony"

sometimes I might be 60% this and 20% that and 20% something else (as we look at our primary "thematic buckets" — and typically people tend to have 3 primary ones, sometimes 4)

while next time I am 80% the "something else" — but leopards don't become canaries and canaries don't show up as tigers there is a core "spiritual truth" to who we are . . . and I believe, very strongly, it keeps coming back, every time

****

it is unlikely that Frederick the Great is a butcher or Einstein a cab driver . . . although that could be part of their evolution as they "develop"

but not where they ultimately land

if people are "working on things", they are working on them whether they have some level of fame or not

what happens is out of our control; what we choose to do, though, is

and it would seem plausible to me that the thing one chooses to do and the drive they exhibit towards achieving it, whether "successful or not"

would speak to the possible inter-connectedness across lifetimes of all separate incarnations

I know lots of people who are celebrities, especially actors and musicians

and they have the same types of issues in many cases as everyone else

and being famous one year does not translate into being

famous or successful the next

yes, I am also super skeptical of Cleopatra or Joan of Arc being housewives today in North Dakota

but . . . there are lots of people who flirt briefly with C list levels of fame

they likely reincarnate, too

****

the question for me is how does "what's within" seek expression

This raises nature/nurture questions which none of us can ever fully define

I think people who have a drive to express some aspect of their "nature"

Likely come pre-loaded with that same drive

How it gets released or expressed

Is tempered by a host of factors, both environmental and genetic (which also invites a lot of speculation about why "these genetics?")

But the thing "within them"

I would suspect

Is always there

****

it seems to me that a drive to "do something" always shows up in people who had careers that we notice

this tendency would, perhaps, continue to carry on — suggesting, perhaps, that an innate drive may be part of the soul essence . . . translated: the emotional template may be the primary thing that "reincarnates"

when we look at defining characteristics that are "consistent" with past life claims

if there is such a thing as reincarnation — and I personally believe there is

then finding "what reincarnates" is pretty important moving forward

my own belief, based on my own home grown ways of looking

is that emotional "styles" will continue — the personality *types* seem to keep going and going, on and on and on

****

another core belief — one I hold strongly . . . is that consciousness is not housed "within the brain"

motor functions may be driven by activity within the brain

but consciousness is "non-local" . . . meaning that it is "around us" and is something we "tap into"

many people, understandably so, will say that everything we "think" is the result of "inserting" information in to the mind through some "absorption pattern": reading, seeing, listening . . . an "experience" that we capture and store

and, if this were true, then yes psychic ability should be impossible

but psychic ability exists . . . I do it all the time and I am, for sure, not the only one

I believe consciousness is something akin to a giant "energy grid" AROUND US

that we tap into much as we might tap into wi-fi at Starbucks

our "access code" to higher and higher "levels" within this grid is (I believe) something we "earn" through various channels

and psychic ability is, looked at from this angle, simply being given greater access codes to information, much like higher and higher levels of Security Clearance by the government

I keep "preaching" that stuff "happens" PRIMARILY because we are in "alignment" with a particular "state of being"

clear your mind of fear, as much as possible, and "allow" yourself to find greater and greater levels of clarity so as to be "in sync" with greater degrees of access to this consciousness "grid"

crazee idea to some — but I believe more and more with
each passing year

that this is "the truth"

****

I also believe (and of course I can't "prove" this, either — but
believe it nonetheless) that ALL "significant" relationships in
your life — whether they last 30 minutes or 30 years

are karmic —

Soul mates, by definition, "change" your life

because, in responding to them, *you* change

and thus, poof, your *path* changes, as well

you may love them, you may be utterly annoyed by them,
or mesmerized or all of the above

but you are never indifferent — soul mates "speak" to your soul

the still small voice where God whispers

and they are a vital part of your evolutionary path

love matters — whether a moment or a lifetime

when you meet one, when your heart dances . . . whether it crashes later or soars

they change your world — and that change, ultimately, is always for the better

****

not all relationships that "don't work" necessarily are "bad", whether that be in this life or a "soul mate" we, somehow, "connect with" from 1365 BC

each of us brings our own bucket of pain; each of us runs the risk of pouring from that bucket

and shattering the safety nets of those we love; it is human nature

love is the arena in which we are least equipped to "succeed" yet it is the arena, too, in which we may find the greatest joy

love those you've loved, even after they have gone

there was a reason you loved them; it didn't go away

your bucket of pain, perhaps, just overflowed and washed away the core of how you loved them

this process runs both directions; their pain, their history, may have blinded them in ways they couldn't fully control and their buckets may have flowed, unimpeded, towards you and washed away their love for you

if we could always stay at a high level, fully awake, our self-esteems fully secure

surely, we would; but that is not always possible

this is a hard one, I know — a lesson with which many of us (me included) struggle; but it is a vital one, as well

forgive, love, move forward

not everything we do is 100% "conscious"; forgive and live to love again

****

Achille Varzi and Ilse Pietsch

Soul mates aren't all love and candlelight; they may show up rock your world and move on

or they may stay . . . and torment you a while longer

not every soul mate is a romance nor is every soul mate who shows up as a romantic partner always an "easy" experience

but they serve a purpose — and that "purpose" is to "change" the emotional and logistical trajectory or your "current path"

****

Sometimes you will find that truly "karmic" relationships

(and yes, I believe there are some that have an extra past life wallop to them)

are always about changing your "frames of reference"

without them, your path goes along on its own trajectory

slow, steady

and then, poof, someone shows up, causes a "reaction"

and sets you off on a different course, with a completely different set of eyeballs

always a blessing — no matter how they appear, no matter what the disruption

some relationships change you more than others — they are always, ultimately, a gift

. . . even if the gift isn't "revealed" until they pass and

the dust settles

****

To me a soulmate is anyone with whom you interact that, due to the emotional "reaction" of your relationship, you see yourself differently and/or make decisions that set you off in a "different direction"

As such, a soulmate is simply a person who shows up and influences you in a dramatic fashion. This might be a romantic partnership (although not all romantic partners, in my eyes, are soulmates), a mentor, or even a rival — if the nature of your relationship and history with this person leads to a change in how you see yourself or what you ultimately "do"

You meet Sally, she shows up, you have a romantic relationship for a year, she leaves and you're exactly the same as 18 months prior . . . Sally was a girl friend, not a soul mate

Then you meet Sarah . . . Sarah shows up, you date her for 3 weeks, but your memories of Sarah linger for 30 years . . . Sarah IS a soulmate

And then you meet Sadie and because of meeting Sadie you decide to transfer schools to be near her and even if you break up a week after going from Ohio State to the University of Illinois, the fact that a profound redirection in your course was "activated" by her presence (and all the new people and/or opportunities — as well as possible "lost opportunities") means (to me) that Sadie is most definitely a soul mate, even if you do everything in your power to avoid seeing her as soon as you break up

Mr. Jones was your high school English teacher; he points out your talents as a writer and helps nurture your talent . . . he is a soulmate

Mr. Smith was your high school football coach; he berates you and then kicks you off the football team . . . a move that has far reaching impacts for years to come in terms of self-esteem and future options (lost scholarship, etc). He, too, is a soul mate

Mr. Brown is a great teacher and you took a class with him every year but you are not fundamentally "changed" (other than an acquisition of knowledge) by attending his classes; Mr. Brown is a good teacher and a positive force in your life — but NOT a soulmate

****

Over the years, I have talked quite a bit about a "unified field" theory of divination. I have tried, in my own way, to forge ahead with my "style" and philosophy as a "reader" and it didn't always connect with other people, in large part because I kept rejecting many of the things they found, in me, most appealing. I understand that — but I was never able to fully articulate what I "did" in a way that I felt was consistent with my "higher self". When I turned the "remote viewer — you're going to get a job in a building next to the fire station" thing on, well . . . all was good.

But that misses the point. The point is . . . root cause.
Without understanding the mechanics of "why" that thing I
see is likely to happen, you are in a passive state, literally asleep.
I am still making my way, slowly — but surely . . . towards
integrating the causal links behind behavior, both backwards
and forwards. The future and the past . . . one unified body of
knowledge, sliced at a specific point — a holographic model of
behavior and pre-cognition with the added bonus of walking
in, and listening to, other "parallel worlds".

The integration of the mind, both conscious and subconscious, with the body . . . and by body I mean not
only the physical body we wear but the larger social, political
body that surrounds us, influencing us in so many ways . . .
bits of energy swirling in, around, and through us . . . the
question: how does the body interface with the mind? How
do we become aware of old psychological triggers in the body;

how do we understand them and make them "conscious" allies as opposed to "unconscious" assassins?

I have always gone after a bigger fish with the expectation that I had all the tools to land the biggest ones. That may not be true but I continue on working towards understanding how it all goes together. I have never given up and I feel somehow closer to "figuring it all out".

I see more and more each day how reincarnation works and why it matters. "Past lives", for me, are the missing link.

I created a divination deck specifically geared towards past lives: the **Khar - Ma: Past Lives Divination Deck** -- and, in doing so, spent quite a bit of time thinking about how past lives might "work". Even more than that, I had additional time to tap in to my own *personal* "karmic vault".

Here is a sample of what I've "discovered".

In the radio shows and live past life "reads" I've done on air, I have talked many times about "thematic buckets" in regards to past life influences. Typically, people have 3 primary themes. Some more, some less but the most common way for me to see it is for people to have 3 primaries; this might be "Healer", "Artist", "Diplomat", "Military", "King", "Spiritual/Monk", "Mystic/Magician", etc etc.

And these "themes" tend to be primary or secondary in a particular life. Someone might be, let's say, 20% Healer, 20% Artist and 60% Builder in this lifetime (relatively speaking) and much like certain planets may work as undercurrents in the natal astrology chart, so too will these "sub-themes" work in the current lifetime, relative to how an individual makes decisions and/or processes information. The ratio might have been much different (and usually that's the case) in a different incarnation as you tend to shift "roles" each round, in order to add texture . . . this allows you to better "see" who you "are", by continually shining your inner spiritual light against this rich and varied tapestry of cumulative experiences.

Not only that, just as the place you live influences how you think and act — native and national cultures seep in to the blood stream, whether you're conscious of it or not — there are also certain places (and the memories of the dominant culture of a particular place) that underscore who you are now — and how you act. The "how you act" part is influenced by an instinctive expectation of "how you SHOULD act" and not only do past life themes "show up", past life "locales" also show up.

If your genetic memory is tuned to a specific channel, say Central Asia, and you're living in West Texas, for example, then you may have a karmic "disconnect" between cultures and attitudes. There is "what you see and hear" and what you "know" deep within. Sometimes they line up; sometimes they don't.

For me, I tend to see myself having 4 primary themes: (1) King / Politician, (2) Mystic / Magician, (3) Military / Rebel and (4) Artist / Aesthete. When I "look" at my own "past lives" I see a LOT of uniforms, a whole lot of uniforms. But I also have the mystic sit in a cave thing going on, too . . . one from each food group :)

I have 4 primary themes, all very strong, which truthfully is fairly unusual, and the themes are, in one way of looking at it, almost polar opposites. One of the outcomes of this type of thematic blending would suggest a fairly "complex" personality (which is kinda true, don't you think) — one at home with sudden and dramatic shifts, in keeping with the natural instinct, and need, for adaptability to potentially shifting sands within the particular "job description" associated with these "types" of lifetimes.

This information can be helpful in defining "styles of learning" as well as "styles of adapting". The ego structure is a fragile beast in all of us and defining and understanding these themes is a good way to delve in to the depth of soul driving us onward. I am not going to go in to a lot of detail in this particular piece, but this "information" is fully accessible (to me anyway and I am sure to others, as well) via something that I can best describe as "home movies in my head".

The lifetime "imprints" somehow on the etheric "film" — which is also how "ghosts" come to be, too, in a slightly different manner. A fascinating subject — one that has driven me onward for over 40 years.

"Every saint has a past and every sinner has a future." — Oscar Wilde

****

People ask me, quite often, "how do I read 'past lives'?"

it comes to me like little movies and then, if I focus a bit more, just like when you watch a movie yourselves, more of the plot line and details start to "come to me"

you can see them, replaying, in a wild tapestry in everyone's etheric field. an amazing little cinematic "trip"

Past Lives are (I believe) quite "real" and investigating past lives is not only an amazing adventure; it is also an incredibly valuable tool for understanding your "current" life :)

it is possible that some of you are "living" in *more* than one "physical body", as we speak

The soul often will split and, as quantum physics suggests (in a slightly different form), soul "fields" will work at a distance from one another — because they are "connected" through a mysterious resonance

The essence of the soul (the etheric "juice") will "experience" living in many different settings and when there is a magnified opportunity to learn in a certain "time period" then the soul will often take on the task of living "flat out" by "splitting" into several physical bodies, concurrently

In which case, you really do live in two (or more) places at one time :)

****

trying to "match" past lives is (for me, at least) a "hunt and peck" process . . . taking specific "clues" and trying to do searches for people who match one piece

and keep going to see if they match "more pieces"

as a result, many times (again, for me) I will think "ok, maybe this one works", only to sit with it for awhile and go "no, I am not sure; I don't think so"

I am not "psychic enough" to have the names and social security numbers just pop in my head; I watch "my movies"

and the movies are not usually "sub-titled"

I wasn't Cleopatra or Joan of Arc, so my possible candidates are a little more "obscure"

yet so far, they all seem to share the "just barely left a minor trace in history (due to standing next to somebody famous); enough that if you keep looking you may find me" thang . . . so I keep on looking !!

I only have the imagery or the emotion or sometimes a "resonance" for a particular time and place (typically, a by-product of "watching the movie")

so — it is safe to say I spend a LOT of time chasing false leads down many a fruitless rabbit hole

but in order to find a rabbit, you still have to look in the hole, anyway

could I be "more productive" doing other things? maybe

but I want to map the territory and, for me, this is the only way I know

****

when it comes to "verifying" a past life — there is no absolute fool-proof way in which this can be done

as a psychic, if I make a prediction that you'll get a job in X type of building or the stock market will do XYZ, that is measurable

it happens or it doesn't — if I say you're this "type" of person and are dealing with XYZ types of "things", that either "rings true" or it doesn't

but with past lives — there is no yardstick with which anyone can say yes / no, that is true

for me, I have spent 40 years — 40 pretty intense years . . . SEARCHING, looking for clues, adding subtracting re-arranging

following dead ends, taking vague snippets and trying to first make a pattern and then find if that pattern "matched" a lifetime — and remember, this has to be a lifetime in which there is actually enough information SOMEWHERE you can find to later use as validation

AND translated or originally in English — since I can't read German, Russian, Hungarian, Persian or any of the other languages most likely to hold information from my personal karmic journey

I have been not only lucky, but super diligent, in tracking down these leads and putting forth "speculative" life times that I feel, for many reasons, may have been ones

in which I have lived before

this isn't done as an ego trip but truly from the standpoint of trying to understand why I "see" the things I see and also from the standpoint of trying to unravel the hows and whys of reincarnation

as it serves as a core component to my personal sense of spirituality and my understanding of God

if reincarnation is "true", well that speaks quite eloquently as to what I need to do in life and what choices are most appropriate

I want to understand what happens when we die, in hopes that it will help me better know how to live

I have also had a lot of help — friends and professionals who I have reached out to over the years who have helped point the way

I am still searching . . . an amazing journey

one unlikely to end anytime soon

Fourteen

Speeding Along

I have been asked, quite a bit, about how I think "Death" works — a subject I (and no doubt many others) find fascinating

my "ideas" (surprise, I know !!) are kind of "at odds" with much of the "common wisdom" of many mediums — who knows who's "right" ??

certainly I make no claims to know anything about capital D "Death" with any "certainty"

but my sense is not that we "go somewhere" when we die but rather we are already, concurrently "somewhere" all along

it is a flip in consciousness, not a journey to "another place" think quantum physics with an electron in two places concurrently. we are both here and "there" and so this connection, which seems so far away, is not so foreign, after all

Achille Varzi and crew, 1930

we don't die to be reborn but are simply wrapped up in a blanket of soul consciousness with many colors, like a tapestry

there is no separation — this is what I am learning

more than ever I believe that we are living concurrently in the "Earth world" and the "Spirit world". I trust more and more that what comes is ok, in its perfect time all is a gift

Death, therefore, isn't really an end

it is simply looking off in to the sunset, focusing on a new day yet to come

****

I believe — can't "prove it" but it is what makes the most "sense to me"

"cellular memories" are stored within the body that are PAST-LIFE driven and it is through the "triggering" of these cellular memories that I believe our "karma" is "initiated"

(which, to me, is a drive or instinct "towards experiences" that will help "refine" our soul "growth" due to the actions we take — and the attitudes and emotions associated with those actions and the "responses" those actions elicit)

so, in English — your need for certain types of "experiences" may be pretty much hard-wired straight from jump

and that drive towards finding whatever within you NEEDS TO BE FOUND

is the primary vehicle through which "karma" and soul "growth" are facilitated

I haven't fully defined the how and why, of course

but, to me, these "past life" memories, if they are physically housed in the body, as I believe they are — perhaps passed on as part of our DNA (how, for example, does it always seem as if people reincarnate looking much the same, with similar body types?)

have to be "housed" someplace and have to be "transported" some how

and if housed within our DNA, as I suspect they are, they are potentially available to all of us to "remember", provided other memories and attitudes don't fully "drown out" these faint echoes from the past

if so, is this thing that reincarnates what we call "the soul"

and is the soul, then, really these memories and instincts hard-wired in to our body through the DNA strands ??

I think, more and more, that perhaps it is

****

I think people "want" to "be here" . . . some of us are "greedy" to live (multiple times)

and want to hop in as many bodies as possible, as often as possible

I know a lot of people say "oh this is my last life" — but I never believe that

. . . it may be true, but I doubt it as I think the goal is not to "get out" (because I think we are "already out" — meaning we are both here "and there" concurrently)

but to savor and explore the possibilities of being "incarnate"

. . . as often as possible

some of you (in my opinion) may actually be living multiple lifetimes RIGHT NOW

is it any whackier that your "soul essence" inhabits 2, 3, or 4 bodies right now rather than just this ONE ??

actually, I think it is ALL pretty incredible

but (to me) "soul splitting" is no more incredible than coming back one at a time

****

if you know "past life energy" you also know current life motivations

and motivation divided by restriction (learned and imposed) equals "your future"

****

it is possible, if not (to me) quite likely . . . that we go though certain "romantic trials" in order to better understand the nature of LOVE and also better understand the specific factors underlying why a person is

. . . as "they is"

so that we can embrace their "stuff" and love them when they need to be loved . . . the most

if such concepts as "soul groups", "soul pods", "soul contracts" and — a term for which my definitions veer sharply from the norm: "soul mates" and . . . "twin flames"

are true . . . it is quite possible that the trains of each can run wild through the forest for years and years only to be brought into alignment through the "help" of their soul "buddies"

who bump into them when they most need to be "bumped"

I am a firm believer in the universe's unicorn being (at least) "half full" not half empty

and I believe the situation I describe above is not only possible . . . but something which happens quite often

and for just the reasons I've outlined

****

In doing all the "exploring" I've done with "Past Lives" over the past 40 plus years, I am inclined to believe

that we live in a universe in which the concept of Unconditional Love is the truth

and ideas about sin, karma, Hell, etc

are not — instead I am inclined to look at these ideas (and the attitudes that come with them) as projections from deep within the psyche that have been made manifest

due to fear

much like a child in a dark room

as we turn on the lights in the bedroom and the dark stops and we can suddenly see there are no boogey men, that it is all ok, so (too) do we lose our fears as we turn on the light within us

I don't believe in an eye for an eye type of karma — we come to learn

we don't come to "pay for our prior sins"

this is my belief

the Earth is like college . . . we come here for specific lessons but to have a chance of "understanding", we have to fulfill certain pre-requisites before being admitted

some major in the Humanities, others in Business or Engineering or Social Work . . . bur we all have certain courses in common before we can earn our degree

as we turn up the wattage on our "inner light" (to me, synonymous with embracing God in whatever way we "do"), we also come closer to seeing

that the universe is ok . . . and we are ok

and that whatever we go through, ultimately, is based in something good and not something designed to punish

this is, also, my belief

that there is a Godly presence and this is not a God who judges

but instead a God who loves

Fifteen

Past Life Guinea Pig

Past Life Research may turn out, ultimately, to be research into "shared consciousness"

The mind is NOT (in my opinion) the source of, nor repository for, consciousness

past lives may turn out to be pods of consciousness — which, translated, means our past life "connections" may be data sets we "align with" through a shared vibratory "signature"

it may be that we've lived before NOT in a one-to-one linear modality but, rather, our conscious "origin" (translated: soul or "spiritual essence") is accessed by multiple physical "Earthly" incarnations in some mad hatter space/time cosmic wi-fi stew

I "believe" in reincarnation but I do NOT believe in a one after another karmic waltz towards "release"

we vibrate at frequencies that are unique, yet "time shared" with others

those "others" are (in my "universe", anyway) our "past lives"

****

sometimes, when I am particularly "quiet", the flashes of "memory" will come to me

they're foreign yet familiar and in that grey area of consciousness between sleep and morning, they come — yet I am fully awake

Achille Varzi, Grand Prix of Nice, 1934

often coming, like now, in the middle of day while doing (and thinking of) something else

but still they are so much aligned with that "state" one thinks of as dreaming — hard to explain but many of you may know this feeling

sometimes, too, when I do readings I will describe, very clearly, what people are planning and when doing this the obvious interpretation is that my vision of their future is a confirmation

but, as I often say to them, it is "possible" that I am simply (in whatever way, however it may transpire) reading their minds

and all the disclaimers are stated out loud

. . . it is in the context of this mind reader / fortune teller "space" that these questions continually come back to me

clear pictures of places and times long ago yet seemingly at my finger tips

are they "mine"? do they "belong" to someone else ??

it is these questions and the very "real" recognition that these fantasy images are, in my world, too often "verifiable"

that make my head spin

these pictures — I "see them"

can practically taste them — they are a special secret spice in my daily stew and when they come, it is like nothing else

a mystery, delicious but elusive

past lives ?? MY past lives ??

or are they "something else" ??

and, if so — what ????

****

the multiplicity of various seemingly "concurrent incarnations" is reflective of overlays with space . . . time is seen as a linear constant

yet the road it travels upon has hills and valleys so the plane has one speed the man on a donkey quite another; attempts to quantify this disparity in "experienced space/time" lead to constructs such as string theory, time folds, etc

I am NOT a physicist and so am coming to similar

"conclusions" not through studying math and physics but through meditation and "searching for past lives"

but my search is pointing me in directions already traveled upon by quantum theorists

what is the MOST super fascinating aspect of my digging into the past life vault is the holographic "construction"

of collected/collective incarnations taken both as a "whole" and as a "singular expression"

this holographic modeling motif is so obvious

when looking at ways in which consciousness and individual "biography" intersect

. . . evolutionary steps mirror prior steps, even if the backdrop and time zones are markedly different, the "perceived experience(s)"

are mirrors

yet aren't

but they possess qualities "mirror-like" and can be experienced as parallel "just alike" experiences

all the while being significantly different yet eerily all the same translated: we don't come back way different from who we were before; we come back with a lot more in common than not

and the mythology of being one thing then and something totally different now

is not my experience of "reincarnation"

space/time "folds", consciousness is non-local, experience and intention not the same thing

we come, to a large degree, "pre-loaded"

and what determines what comes into the load is a reflection of what's always been in the cosmic warehouse

a company that makes washing machines doesn't ship yachts or Ferraris

it ships washing machines

we can be in more than one place at a time but we can't (if my interpretation of what I am "seeing" is correct)

be two different "things"

****

there has to a reciprocity in "response" between the wave and the cell this is how (in my opinion)

the karmic blueprint/template

#starts

this is also one of the potential benefits of past life "matching"

creating a wave "relationship"

between the past life and current incarnation

a rapid-fire way to "re-awaken"

dormant potential

****

I think we will find that what reincarnates is akin to an electro-magnetic field — and our consciousness is simply "tuning in" to the field . . . leading to cellular "construction" of the body

a weird hodge-podge transmission of DNA and "radio waves"; there has to be something that reincarnates and it has to get from somewhere into the body, somehow someway

I believe wave harmonics are the "transfer agent" — which leads to a secondary prediction . . . healing in the future will be done via genetic "regeneration" accomplished by a vehicle of some sort that is capable of emitting high level directed wave patterns, which will influence cellular regeneration, much like rebooting your laptop to its original state

you want to, basically, set off a means for harmonizing between the wave function of the past life

and now

so as to re-calibrate cellular regeneration within the current body

****

Most people, I believe, see God as "other" because they see Death as "other"

when I die I go "somewhere" — so the question of God is always rooted in this question of what is "around the corner"

what happens when the body "stops" ??

I believe that reincarnation is the way in which the cycle "loops" and, as such, there is no actual death but rather a continual "re-alignment"

I also don't see consciousness as being "housed within" the brain, hence "captured" within the physical body

consciousness is, basically, an alignment with/through a pervasive etheric energy, God and all prima materia one thing, with different flavors seen through a prism, a holograph of which we often are ill placed to fully see

when you stop seeing Death as "going somewhere"

and realize you're both "here and there" all at once

then your world will change

and your fear of Death will stop

no one wants to Die because the party's happening here, right now

I don't want to stop — somebody truly rockn may walk through the DOOR

but there is no "other" place, nor "other" state of being

life and death are in alignment no different — simply light and dark sides of a golden moon

when you see that you have one foot in the Spirit world right now and Life / Death are tape loops not either/or

then you will feel more content, more in love

more . . . everything

Enzo Ferrari + Achille Varzi (center), standing behind Giuseppe Campari in his Alfa Romeo 1750 6C Compressore

truth . . . there is no "there"

there

it is ALL within

****

When people are ready to be POWERFUL — then they will BE powerful

until then, they will continue to create "situations" in which crisis follows crisis and the crisis is purposeful in that it gives them something "to do"

as well as a convenient excuse not to be

powerful

patterns are habits until they are transmuted into lessons — lessons are painful reminders until they are transmuted into meaningful "information"

and that information ultimately is jet fuel towards acquiring power / mastery

this works within one lifetime or across ALL LIFETIMES

it's up to you

patterns "repeat", in the simplest way I can say it . . . until you are "ready to stop"

Sixteen

Mirror Mirror on the Past Life Wall

I have speculated that all past lives will show very strong physical characteristics in common with the current incarnation; they don't have to be twins, but they should have lots of pieces/parts that jump out as "like one another" . . . "oh, Andrew looks just like dear old Uncle Puffnstuff", that kind of thing

contrary to what anyone may say, ALL past life matches are guesswork (including my own) and no one knows, nor can anyone "prove" ANYTHING about past lives

That, however, does not stop us from speculating and theorizing and HUNTING

and the hunt is quite a little journey

I have, over the many long years of needle pulling from assorted haystacks, found people who (a) looked like me, (b) matched many of the story elements I "remembered", and (c)were just waiting (so it seemed at the time; fingers crossed, fingers CROSSED) there patiently for me to find them

As FATE would have it, I began to find multiple people who fit a, b, and c and so . . . complications developed

After having no one, occasionally I would end up with multiples

And, psychic pedigree or no, it is still detective way work more than omniscience

I had to "test-drive" my past life matches

Only to later, more often than not, throw them back into the creek

Which means I have found answers only to later realize I stopped too soon

Drats, foiled again

And the hunt picks up and continues

****

in looking at "past lives", what I look for are certain kinds of "themes" psychological "patterns", instinctive styles for dealing with one's emotions

and behavioral "predispositions"

these basic psychological signatures will play out over and over and the style typically remains pretty much the same — the situations and the "responses" to those situations

are the things that "evolve"

. . . sooooo, in looking at my "own style" I always see a really interesting duality — part of me (both in terms of personality and actual "past lifetimes") gravitates towards wild child artist types

while another "part" of me gravitates to military academies and professional careers in the military

an interesting mix . . . but I believe past lives (and the "healing" and integration of the collective sum of all lives "lived") can be "brought together"

within one's current lifetime

in other words, one can (not easy, but possible) bring all the various bits and pieces (lifetime by lifetime) from ALL the prior incarnations into "alignment" right now

this "duality" of artist / wild child and professional soldier

(along with a large dose of two other "themes": religious / spiritual and king / politician)

is (in my opinion) one of the key drivers as to WHY I study past lives with such intensity

understanding the mystical spiritual as revealed by/through/with "past lives"

satisfies not only the artist and mystic — it also speaks to the warrior / king "parts"

because Religion is too often used as a political weapon

and to be free of the tyranny of someone "using Religion" to keep others in the dark, so as to control their behavior

through controlling the cognitive frameworks driving their thinking — and thus driving their value system and decision making

is the greatest gift anyone can "give"

to understand past lives is to be free of Spiritual Tyranny

the truth, quite literally, will "set you FREE"

The winners of Mille Miglia, 1934 . . . Achille Varzi and mechanic Amedeo Bignami driving this Alfa Romeo 8C 2600

****

All the "is it possible I was Marilyn Monroe" seekers are sharing a thought that serves some deeper purpose . . . my "understanding" of myself — seen in the juxtaposition of possible past life matches (the people on the internet I so breathlessly contemplate for a moment or a year as "me — then / maybe")

is enriched by the process of hunting and "comparing"

those lives that touch us as stories that perhaps we shared . . . and the cognitive sparks that fly from attempting to understand what it "all means"

also serve a valid and important purpose

there is a functional value to this process of self-examination; each (possible) past life a mirror in which to see one's self

each peak a window into how God operates

and the process of searching for God and searching for past lives and searching for myself — three ways of saying the exact same thing

changes me and changes my "consciousness"

and gives me fuel to do the things I do, with ever increasing ease and clarity as the years roll by

as a psychic

they're all "connected"

just as we are all connected with one another and all the other living organisms here and elsewhere

past lives are real; but the individual "current lifetime" that we think we know, as our baseline to find lives lived "before"

is probably limited

we see past lives as things that "happened" and God as a human somewhere else that looks like here, only without trash and old age but it may be that past lives and this life are concurrent pulses of consciousness

all interconnected, the red light blinking all the time

past lives may not be past

since consciousness (another way of saying "the soul")

is not #confined to the body

the young girls wanting to be the reincarnation of Marilyn Monroe are finding something of themselves

because they are seeing aspects of self

in the blending of self with "not-self"

consciousness does not stop and start within us

and that is why this process of hunting for past lives is so absolutely

positively gloriously

#MAGICAL

****

Studying past lives, ultimately, is about forgiveness . . . forgiving God, forgiving events

. . . forgiving yourself

Love is the thing that comes with you; people show up over and over

and the breath of God is always near you

this is what I have learned after all these years of seeking "the past"

seeing it allows you to really see your truth

make peace with it . . . and in finding that peace

ideally make the world a better place

because you're better

****

karma" is your "faulty understanding" of cause and effect, grounded in old hurts and "inappropriate" means for dealing with your pain

or guilt — for inflicting pain on others

as such, it is often the root cause of both emotional and/or physical "ailments"

understanding "the past" and forgiving yourself are key

components in releasing the "dis" ease

and healing

past lives, as a result, are the key to everything

it may not seem this way . . . but, deep down, it is the root of all "issues"

find the root cause, apply "healing" at the root

and the pain will start to dissolve

****

one of the concepts I am working on — as both a "past life" theoretician and (hopefully) a "practical" helper

in facilitating personal growth for others (as well as myself)

is to look at "past" and current lifetime(s) as a potential "cluster"

. . . meaning there is a reciprocal two way street relationship between them

they (literally) impact each other

and even though history is static, "meaning" is fluid

and in the inter-dimensionality of spiritual energy . . . fixing something today can also help re-align actions (and intentions) from the past

was this event a disaster . . . or a catalyst for growth

this works not only in your current lifetime . . . but in your lifetime "stack", too

you can heal multiple lifetimes all at once — provided you "understand"

and move forward

knowledge is good, no matter how long it may take

it is still

. . . good

and worthwhile

****

in "concurrent life times" all lives "being led" are singular and unique yet they all LINK BACK TO a single, higher external source

This linkage to the soul essence is what connects the individual lifetimes

this *soul essence* from which each lifetime "springs" is like data housed in "google cloud"

In this particular visual model, the body is the laptop and the essence stored in the cloud is "consciousness"

Time, from the vantage point of the soul essence, is *folded*

For each individual lifetime, though, the experience will appear, and be perceived as, linear in the sense that one lifetime "happened" historically before the other

but the conscious connection to a higher source is NOT linear

meaning that each individual linear body will have full access to a singular source

that is being "shared"

translated: the soul "essence" (source), as I mentioned above, sees them in folds

But the individual lifetimes perceive the connection though as a straight line

your spirit / soul essence is a single thing

every life and every physical body has a one to one relationship with this singular essence

but the essence can permeate multiple bodies at what may appear to be the "same time" because from the perspective of the essence there is NO LINE

so the essence permeates ALL lives

but the individual singular lives are all "different"

Even though they share this singular root

Each person from a particular essence will come with the same types of talents, predispositions — always

So if you have artistic ability this time round, you had it before

If you are highly verbal, you were highly verbal (in one way or another)

#before

Each lifetime is different — because the body is different, the era in which you live is different, the DNA is slightly different

and the individual astrology chart is different

But the soul essence is constant

And this constant source influences (and conversely is influenced by) each individual incarnation

and this, to me, is how past lives can work if we try and

imagine past lives as happening side by side in the same calendar year

****

my belief is that there is an explanation (somewhere) within time/space modeling that will shed light not only on how time "works"

but how consciousness can be expanded within the individual

at seemingly 'quantum speed"

to understand where the source "is"

is to have access to, in theory, unlimited levels of information

and processing speeds intellectually not normally perceived as possible

my theories about past lives are partly about past lives

but, more importantly, about how to "get good" at things

at lightning speed

****

it is understandable that we see our bodies and our current "lifetimes" as a finite singular entity we live we die

I personally do not believe this is true — call it "channeled", a vision, whatever you wish

it keeps "coming to me", over and over, that we are high vibratory (and by high vibration, I mean vibrating quickly, not, necessarily, some "elevated, lofty spiritual" place)

creatures

although I believe we ARE lofty elevated spiritual essences, each and every one of us

these "spiritual essences" (the "who" of who we are) exist in multiple places concurrently

yet are joined as singular vibratory forces, all the same

if this is so, then Death is not an end but rather a vibratory switch in speed

because we are both here AND THERE all the time

and much like the kitchen table is in actuality a bunch of molecules both independent and working together at the same time, rather than simply big blocks of wood screwed together

so, too, Death is a minor change in vibrational "direction"

the kitchen table could catch fire and no longer look like a kitchen table — it "died" to that function and form

the energy "transformed" during the fire and went somewhere else . . . yet the table "essence" underscores "where it went"

and "where it went" was connected, in terms of vibration, also with where it came from

before it collectively "assembled" into a kitchen table

meaning — we are already IN the place we go when we die, right now

the forms may change, the arrangement seemingly will "re-arrange"

but the finite form of the kitchen table, if viewed at its core, was never what it "appeared" anyway

. . . taking this a step further then, "past lives" (to me) are legit

(based on this logic, too) as they (seen in this context)

are simply clusters of vibrations acting BOTH as singular elements and concurrent harmonic patterns

like the kitchen table that lived for a time as a tree and, after burning, transformed into different forms of energy the burnt wood later fertilized perhaps new growth, a new tree or plant

so past lives are sort of separate and not separate, all at the same time

just as quanta of energy are both here and there all at the same time, even though supposedly it is impossible

controlled experiments suggest this is the actual "truth"

sounds sort of nutty, I know — but quantum physics also sounds nutty

bottom line — long story short

WE DON'T DIE

our vibratory patterns "re-arrange" as part of an evolutionary journey

driven by who knows what for God knows what reason :)

still, I believe more and more with each passing day

that Death, as we conceive of it, is not true

the essence remains, a constant

forms "seem different" and vibrate with or against other

forms

based on harmonic resonance patterns (throw a pebble into the creek)

but the song, basically, always remains the same

Achille Varzi, French Grand Prix, 1931

Seventeen

God is My Co-Pilot

why do I care soooooo much about past lives? in addition to helping me learn about, and "deal" with, any psychological complexities within my own life

it has also helped me move into a "peaceful space" with the idea of my death — I am (after all) on the plus side of 60

and so far I have already shot past, long past, the longevity of every past life I have uncovered as well as my own father

so lively as I am . . . Death may not be that far off, either

but even more importantly (to me) is the idea that my "work" with past lives (and what they might "mean") may help others

deal better with their own emotional trials and also find

a harmony within themselves

that allows them to make choices based on who they are rather than being railroaded into choices that aren't optimal

because of pervasive cultural constructs — such as this limiting viewpoint being rammed down everyone's throats

of a God that "judges"

this is simply not true . . . holding visions of a God who only likes one group doing things one way is not "reality"

we have choices . . . yet there are "Natural Laws" always at work, most of which we are unaware

my goal in sharing my past life journey is to help people find themselves, so they have more freedom to make choices in harmony with who "they are"

and, as a result, skyrocket the probability they will find

personal happiness

****

people "come back" and they don't come back just one after the other

I realize it is a leap of "logic" to see how it would be possible to live, let's say, in 3 different bodies at the same time — all

doing different things

the hurdle for this is an associative drive to equate the BODY with the soul or essence

it's not . . . the soul essence is a vibratory pattern — basically a wave function that reflects light

Achille Varzi in his Alfa Romeo at the 1930 Targa Florio

yeah . . . not what you might expect

and this wave function interacts with (and ABSORBS) denser vibratory patterns that are functionally in alignment with its "direction"

this functional alignment is the driving mechanism through

which cells "come together" to make a body

but the vibratory pattern can exist as a holographic beam in multiple places because there is no functional deterrent to light particles

existing in "concurrent places" (a function of space/time and the density of what the light "passes through")

these light patterns then "reflect" off a bigger source — call this God, the universe, whatever you like . . . this "bigger source" drives the manner in which the beams coalesce and the bodies take form

due to the ways in which light is reflected and cells (light packets) "combine"

and yeah, I know your heads are spinning

but think of it this way . . . bodies are composites of light beams wrapped up within cells

and the light within the cell has an origin and it also reflects based on what it "hits"

if this is true — then the light can (by being projected through a "universal prism") BOUNCE off multiple sources at what appears to the naked eye

to be

exactly the same time

so consciousness sees the events concurrently because they are later RECORDED as having "existed" concurrently

the ordering of the interaction post fact is the organizing principle on which history (and historical consciousness) is based

we write it down that it happened this way; therefore it happened this way

maybe maybe not

we are light beams, pure and simple

combined into patterns seen through a prism

and yeah I believe in reincarnation as the ultimate espression of this "reflection"

of the original source

****

"Dual incarnations" are further evidence (in the sense in which we can take this concept as evidentiary) of the interconnectedness of "matter"

and the underlying fabric of consciousness that overlays corporeal "reality" . . . concepts such as the akashic records and non-locality of consciousness

are actually *opportunities* for self-healing; the brain is not the home of consciousness . . . GOD is consciousness and consciousness is GOD and we can see, feel, + experience this connectedness

once we embrace the idea that all is #connected

knowing this also must convince us that we are never fully alone

this knowledge will change our sense of self

and changing how we see ourself

changes *everything* else

#LOVE

****

if there is no "finality" in Death (with a Capital "D") — as I've said, I believe we have a foot in "both worlds" all the time

. . . then perhaps there is "overlap" between "past lives" and our current lifetime

maybe we come back to heal old hurts and find joy where joy was nowhere to be found

I don't believe in "karma" as retribution or punishment

I do, however, believe it is possible to "fly in two lifetimes" at once — to find and share beauty in both lifetimes

a tie-in . . . I believe this

Achille Varzi driving for Auto Union, 1935

I believe we can heal ourselves and this healing goes back to prior lifetimes, too

what we learn, and how we "choose to live" . . . can make the "prior" lifetime take on even greater meaning

****

not all things that "haven't worked" in your world (including

161

"past lives") are necessarily "bad" as they may have served as a backdrop for you in which you could more easily understand things that will "help you" later on

or they were perhaps a chronological "place holder" gently nudging you into the "right place right time"

also helping ensure you had a certain core understanding of "who you are" when that "right place right time" finally showed up :)

however, I think it is always important to look forward, with the most positive attitude possible, with the highest expectations possible

beating yourself up is not in your best interests — maybe it "served a purpose" but ultimately that purpose can only be realized

once you flip the switch and start doing things and thinking about things

in ways that will lift you up, not tear you down

the pain is purposeful — but no fun

I choose fun . . . and choose, as much as possible, to learn from past pain

so as to maximize the probability of future "pleasure"

it's a choice — although not all choices are "conscious"

as your consciousness "expands", so, too, the "control" of your choices

pain was positive if it helps you re-align for later . . . but why live in pain

this is the "switch" we are all seeking to flip

and more than anything, helping people find this switch is what "I do"

****

much as sometimes we "need" to go into our own 40 Days of "Emotional Wilderness" in order to better understand "who we are"

. . . so to better understand "what best to do"

not only for the logistics of our future life, but also to move more fully into alignment with bunnies, unicorns, and our "happy space"

we also may find, for many of us, the bleed-through with other lifetimes also serves its purpose as a light bulb in a dark room

pointing us towards attitudes more commensurate with a "fuller integration" of the emotional foundation and spiritual foundation most compatible

with bunnies and unicorns

in other words, we can tap into "past life awareness" as a tool

to better understand what drives our "emotional response patterns"

because, Law of Attraction etc etc

the only way to change our lives . . . is to change our thinking

and the only way really to change our thinking

is to understand, on some level

(a) what "drives it"

and (b) why that mode of thinking "may not work" as we, ideally, might like

. . . there is a lot of information and a lot of potential "power"

sitting in the closet, waiting to be worn like a new coat

past lives, current lives, life death all of it

they don't happen "all at once"

but the spiritual essence, the spiritual sub-atomic quanta (if you will)

IS everywhere all at once

both here AND THERE

and while our limited cognitive faculties miss the dog whistle most times from other "lives lived"

that energetic pulse

beats on

you can find the Rosetta Stone of what makes you tick

through exploring this past life quanta

the little neutrinos of God's Light

pass along unnoticed

but they carry all within them even though they are tinier than the tiniest thing you might imagine

****

thinking drives action

but no one understands what drives thinking

so theoretically (and, to me, actually, as well) no one understands why people "do what they do"

one person may do the same consistent thing 99.998% of the time and then — poof

a change, out of left field

past lives may seem as if they are "unconscious"

but it is not so much they are unconscious as much as they are restricted by the lack of "proper words" to describe

what we see . . . and much as Language drives cognition (what we call something in large measure determines what we "think about it")

so too does this lack of an adequate way to talk about past life "memories" limit our conscious understanding

however, there are tools (much like the tools physicists use to study atomic energy) that we have available to us

that allow us to slow down the rates of oscillation of these past life neutrino buds

and, in slowing down the cognitive drivers of an individual, we can both (a) see and (b) interact with these sub-atomic "past life quanta"

why is this "important" ??

just as playing with small little bits of "invisible energy" allowed scientists to develop the most powerful explosives ever known and tap into energy sources never before imagined

the same holds true here

by tapping into this "resource" we can unlock the "collective power" of this "accumulated wisdom"

****

we tend to think of ourselves as individuals — rather than a host of cells and living "parts"

so too do we tend to see ourselves as singular "lifetimes" rather than a collection of experiences bound together (different names, different places . . . yet all working together, just like the individual cells within the body)

and the image of each life as a singular cell within a "greater body" might help make more clear

the concept of multiple, concurrent

lifetimes

time seems as if it goes in a straight line but go "fast enough" .

. . and it appears to curve, as light plays tricks (or so it seems)

yet if we are "bodies of light" isn't this to be "expected"

reincarnation is the *truth* — and it is both simpler and more complicated than most can accept, or imagine

but the analogy of cells within the body and lifetimes collected within the "soul essence"

is a legit comparison

****

the question continually comes up (*what we talked about earlier in the chapter entitled "Biometrics"*)

as to whether I believe there is a "physical resemblance"

between your "current" life and your "past" lives

. . . I have written many articles over the years about my "theories" as to the "transmission" of the spiritual essence

from one lifetime to another . . . and in that "transmission" — because if Reincarnation is true, then no matter how little we may know about it

we can say with some level of confidence that (a) there has to be a means of getting "something" from the old body into the NEW body and (b) the "thing" (whatever that may be) that gets "transmitted"

has to have some properties that would "reflect" that connection

. . . ALL talk about Reincarnation is theoretical — no one knows, not me

nor anyone else

I know what I know but I am not 100% positive I even "know that"

ontology meets metaphysics (as in "New Age" metaphysics)

. . . my belief is that there is a confluence between DNA and astrology; what I have called "Astro-Genetics"

and these two elements are "drivers" of behavior, because they influence the "state of being" of the individual in such a way as to gently steer the individual down the road

long story only sort of long, I think there will always be a physical resemblance of one sort or another

a beautiful woman one round may be not so beautiful the next, yet will still sort of look the same

I think that "still sort of look the same" thang

is always gonna be there, on some level

many will dispute this; in fact they have already hahahahaa

this may be due to the disputer having found a lifetime as Queen Esmerelda of Lichtenstein and even though there is not the slightest hint of actual "resonance" between the two

somehow the identification has been made and the "truth" defined

. . . again, no one knows

no one

and because I say it, for sure doesn't make it "true"

no matter how much I may think my arguments the most persuasive ever formulated

. . . the memories, the "essence", the DETAILS drive the "hunt"

I have thought I was so many so and so's over the years only to dig deeper and see the connections were surface level only

there was a "vibe" and common elements

but they, on further, deeper review, didn't hold up

bottom line, I do think there likely IS a physical resemblance between all the lifetimes lined up together

just because I spent 40 years searching like a madman frantically looking

and then, suddenly, found someone who had all the elements I was looking for (and conversely, hardly anyone else possibly could)

and is my pretty much literal *twin* — someone who looks sooooo much like me that I could easily say "oh these are stills from a movie I did when I was in my early 30's"

doesn't "prove" reincarnation

but perhaps, like Twain's famous line about history: 'History doesn't repeat itself, but it does rhyme"

we might say the same about past lives

Achille Varzi, Argentina, 1947

somehow, the collective lifetimes all RHYME with one another, in fairly distinctive (and usually quite obvious) ways

****

one of the beauties — and certainly unexpected byproducts . . . of digging in the past life vault all these many years

is the RECOGNITION that we have ALL, at one time or another, done some AMAZING THINGS

so, if we have done it once, or twice, or 6,218 times

. . . we can also, right now, in THIS LIFETIME

do it AGAIN

this is the greatest lesson I have learned after devoting almost 40 years to this crazee needle in the tiniest haystack search

. . . and now, this lesson is my greatest power

so, too, it could be for you, as well

Eighteen

Fast Times at Deadwood High

Achille Varzi ultimately returned to the racetrack, after the Second World War ended. He was 40 years old; effectively, the prime years of his career (age 32-40) were tossed aside . . . a combination of those seasons lost while in the throes of addiction coupled with the years when all racing in Europe stopped (late 1939-1945) due to the war. But the rehab, the lost years, the "stigma", none of it stopped him from getting back in a car when racing resumed at the end of World War II and doing his thing, and doing it remarkably well.

Varzi came back, raced (and won) in South America, attempted to qualify (which he failed to do) for the 1946 Indianapolis 500, and was winning races once again on the same tracks in Europe that he had raced on years earlier, his results much like before when he was considered one of the top drivers in the world.

His up and down affair with Ilse was over and he rekindled his relationship with his girlfriend before Ilse, Norma Colombo, marrying her and settling in to a less intense, seemingly very workable, life until tragedy struck at Bremgarten in 1948.

The affair with Ilse, though, had been red hot; a passionate fiery romance with more twists turns and roadblocks than a Lifetime Movie Night marathon. Varzi's *name* was important in Italy during the 1930's and so other forces, led by Mussolini, stepped in to block Ilse from entering Italy to be with her man. Ilse was literally banned from entering the country and the relationship died, but not without a fight. Was this all at once or little by little, a series of emotional "deaths" one upon another? Who knows. This is an abridged version of the romance, of course, and the true nature of their feelings for each other we'll likely never know.

Louis Chiron + Achille Varzi, winners of The French Grand Prix,
1931

But if Varzi "was like me", then the passion he felt for her was real and perhaps (like me, as well) the intensity of his feelings pushed everything else onto the back burner. Moderation is not, historically, one of my key attributes and for a race driver with a burning competitive nature like Varzi, moderation was likely not one of his key attributes either.

Concurrent with Varzi and Ilse's affair in 1935, illicit and something no one wanted, was another coupling of a driver for Auto Union, one that would soon be promoted as, pretty much, THE Nazi "Dream Couple".

Bernd Rosemeyer was Varzi's teammate and, upon winning the 1935 Czechoslovakian Grand Prix (a race in which the fastest lap was recorded by Achille Varzi, who was forced to retire due to gearbox issues after leading most of the race), he was introduced on the winner's podium to the famous German aviatrix, Elly Beinhorn.

A handsome blonde with an exceptional talent as a driver, Bernd was a member of the SS with the rank of *Hauptsturm-führer,* equivalent to an Army Captain in the U.S. Bernd and Elly quickly became a couple after that first meeting and were promoted as the perfect German celebrity duo; the two elicited a very different public reaction than the one shown to Ilse and Achille. Both romances were happening, live and 3D, at the same time.

Bernd/Elly = good, Achille/Ilse = not good.

Bernd was seen by many as "the perfect Nazi", a perfect Aryan specimen in every way and Achille was well . . . just not. But Bernd was a complicated guy who, like Varzi, was more interested in cars than politics, more interested in love than ideology.

Still, Rosemeyer understood the benefits that came with

being a Nazi Poster Boy and therein a tale doth lie. Charming, charismatic, good looking with a beautiful young wife and a trophy as the European Champion, he had quite a bit in common, in some ways, with Tazio Nuvolari. When I look at his photos, I feel a conflicted kind of energy — he is appealing and annoying, all at the same time. There has to be (I believe) a sub-plot to this story that would cause me to *react* in the way in which I do whenever I see a photo or hear his name.

Teammates often have conflicts and Bernd (who was a relative newcomer to auto racing, having been a champion motorcycle racer) was winning more races than Achille Varzi, a seasoned and highly publicized (and highly paid) professional with a history of success driving automobiles. Is this because he was the better driver or because, perhaps, he had mechanical assistance on his car not offered to Varzi? Again, a question without easy or easily verifiable answers although my suspicion is that Bernd Rosemeyer was a true generational type of talent — all the pieces/parts falling into place for a "more here than meets the eye" type of relationship between two men striving to be "the best".

My suspicion is that Varzi was not really down with the Nazi SS hoopla and Bernd Rosemeyer (and all the others) may have been a bit of a challenge for Achille in his time with Auto Union. My guess is their Facebook relationship status would have been "it's complicated".

The famous rivalry is Varzi - Nuvolari but these two were friends. They had "spats", they broke up for a time (or two) but, deep down, their's was a love match, one of mutual respect and genuine mutual affection. Varzi - Rosemeyer, though, I believe was a *very* different kind of relationship.

When I look at photos of the great drivers of the time:

Campari, Chiron, Carraciola, Stuck, Moll, et al I have distinctly different but equally powerful reactions to each of them. When I look at Nuvolari, I feel love, I feel happy. I certainly don't feel that way when I look at photos of most of the German drivers, most especially don't feel a "happy vibe" with Stuck and Rosemeyer. I "like them" (kind of) but I don't "trust them".

Do these impressions mean anything? Well, who knows. But when I try to get into a quiet contemplative space to "think back" to when I might have been in another body driving cars 180 mph with a cloth helmet and no seat belt, I feel this tightness and *duality* of purpose when thinking of Stuck and/or Rosemeyer. Which face do they show me?

And the wheels on the past life race car go . . . where, exactly?

Achille Varzi, winner of the 1934 Nice Grand Prix

A "man's man", racing cars at speed, defying death, seen constantly with a string of beautiful admiring women by his side — this picture comes with a canned narrative. Bernd Rosemeyer fit this image; Achille Varzi fit it, as well. But is the stereotype always true? Was Varzi perhaps a much more sensitive soul than the ambitious, politically savvy Rosemeyer, someone who raced just because he loved it and who didn't fit the conventional picture of what a race driver was supposed to be?

Is it possible that Varzi was unable to tune out what he saw with Hitler and the Fascists in Italy — much like an athlete today not going along with President Trump? This plotline is never presented and it may be my own personality overlayed on Varzi and not, of course, be "the truth". But is it possible? And if it *is* possible, is it also possible that some of the things said about him were presented in such a way as to diminish Varzi's truth (by impugning his character, first) if his feelings *were* to be known? If this were true, is it equally possible this was done because he had something to say that wouldn't have been convenient for others, if allowed to say it?

****

We'll never know the answer to the questions posed above. What I do know, though, is that I, personally, have a very real innate understanding of the 1930's in Germany in a visceral way that likely most who weren't there do not and I am acutely attuned to anything that *reminds* me of this time in any way. I *remember* Germany in the 1930's.

This memory is not normal, not easily quantified nor explained . . . I think these memories, these emotional time bombs, are *past life* memories and much as I've tried to see this from every conceivable angle, in my limited ways of analyzing my own truth, this is the answer that makes the most sense to me. Somehow, I was there. Somehow.

****

Remote viewing, collective unconscious, Astral travel . . .

maybe? But somehow I remember it.

```
Why I might remember it has been a fire underneath
me all these many years as I feverishly try to
understand it.

Memories of actually "being there", having lived
through something emotionally quite intense, lead me
to surmise the strong possibility that I was there
and my experiences, and what is left after the
experience, perhaps traumatized me in such a way
that I can't fully move past them.
```

This is *the answer* I circle back to every time — the experience was just *too much . . .* and it was REAL.

This may NOT have been Varzi, though. I could have a valid past life memory of Berlin in 1935 and been someone else. Or, what I think is the REAL ANSWER, I may have "split" and lived two *concurrent* lifetimes who *each* lived for a time in Germany during the 1930's — Varzi and another person, still running loose somewhere without proper ID, unwilling to show him or herself and thus serving to add another layer of complexity to this crazee Madhatter Tea Party scavenger hunt. Is it any wonder I'm often confused by it all?

****

Since Varzi seemed fine, on the surface at least, in the late 1940's, does that negate the likelihood that *his* experiences were the ones I'm remembering that were so traumatic as to "leave a mark" next time round?

We could get into a discussion of high functioning people

suffering depression or PTSD or open a Pandora's box filled with all manner of sidebar Freud on speed dial puzzles . . . Monday Morning Quarterbacks.

Bottom line: I don't have *answers* to any of these questions. As I warned in my introduction, this is a travelogue of how I went *looking* for answers and I can't promise a neat little package at the end of the show with all the loose ends explained, definitive proof the butler really did it.

As an example, the answer to the question "did I live in Germany in the 1930's?" may have a "yes" answer and the secondary question "was I Achille Varzi?" be "no". There is no absolute way of knowing what's true. NO PAST LIFE can ever with 100% certainty "be confirmed". This, too, plagues me and drives me in my quest to find answers and understand who I am, now, and how I "got here".

Tazio Nuvolari, Varzi's friend and rival (and his replacement as a team driver for Auto Union) being congratulated on his victory by Adolf Hitler

This memory has been the bugaboo of my existence all these years — the coal in my engine driving me on looking for answers. The fact that Varzi drove for Germany, drove for Hitler, and then had *issues* . . . I find this piece of the Varzi puzzle more than a wee bit intriguing. But, as I mentioned earlier, it's possible (a) I was someone other than Varzi or (b) I was both Varzi and a mystery guest, still in hiding as well as (c) I'm an idiot and don't know what I'm talking about.

Again, I offer no answers, only more questions. But these are directed questions and I have my theories, nonetheless.

Getting back, though, to Varzi . . . What do the highlight reels from Varzi's life tell me about *who I am*, if anything? Is there something (provided we approach the analysis from the standpoint that I may very well be the real, quite literal, reincarnation of this man) that I might find in his life story that perhaps sheds some light on my own?

****

There are several odd bits of synchronicity in my early life that, in retrospect, may be significant (or not) in tying the loose ends together. In the early 1970's, when the car maker Alfa Romeo was on the ropes and effectively non-existent, I always (for some unknown reason) was drawn to them and saw them as the "best car". As a child, when the Miss Universe pageant was on TV, my pick, every year, was always "Miss Italy". And when asked, as a high school senior, what I wanted "to be" after high school — my long-term vocational goal, my answer was "racing driver". I am not a winter sports person, at all, but I have always, since childhood, (for some reason) wanted to do bobsledding. Varzi was a captain, it appears, for Italy's

184

Olympic Bobsledding team in 1936 !!

I always, too, had this odd romantic notion of being a champion who "returned from the scrap heap" and was a winner, again, after being "written off". A strange notion, perhaps, for a boy in Junior High School.

There are lots of these little blips and taken together perhaps they weave a wild tapestry of oddities and wonders. I feel a contentment with the pictures in my head now, a sense of peace with the idea that I may have lived in this tumultuous time in History, with so much promise followed by so much destruction, the world turned upside down by zealots and madmen.

I have learned a lot over the years searching in my wild Frankenstein's monster way to find the switch to make the pictures be a comfort and not a source of confusion. I found God, found serenity, found a purpose in following where these pictures in my head took me.

****

I am at peace *now* with Achille Varzi — and the notion I may have been this magical man doing all these magical things in a magical but totally topsy turvy time (proof or no proof), at peace with the 1930's, at peace with "failure", at peace with loves lost, and (most importantly, I think) at peace with *Death*.

I will never know for sure if I am the reincarnation of Achille Varzi; never know with 100% certainty if there is a God or an afterlife or if any of the other things I've talked about in this book are true. But I have a strong FAITH they're true. A complete and absorbing belief in God, in Reincarnation, in the notion of Love and a divine purpose to life and living. It's good to be here. It's *good* to be alive !!

It wasn't always this way (for me) but my cup is 7/8 full now at all times. Exploring past lives and connecting to what this search for answers (ultimately a search for God) has shown me changed my world. I know things now I couldn't possibly have figured out when I started. I have a sense of being, finally, "in the right place", a sense of being *connected* to something higher

than myself, a sense of being in sync with a higher "purpose".
Peace. Finally. Peace, too, with myself . . . after *years* of going
to war.

   Not such a bad place to be . . . after all.

Nineteen

A Racing Legacy

My Personal "Top Ten" favorite drivers are (not surprisingly I guess): #1), Achille Varzi, #2) Stefan Bellof, #3) Ayrton Senna, #4) Tazio Nuvolari, #5) Jim Clark, #6) Danica Patrick, #7) Jochen Rindt, #8) Peter Revson, #9) Lewis Hamilton, and #10) Steve McQueen.

Danica is more than just a pretty face and Steve McQueen was way more than "just an actor". These are my personal favorites and, to me, they're a formidable, ubertalented, and totally badass group.

I want to talk a little bit, though, about my father, who is a key piece to this interlocking past life puzzle . . . and thank him, too, for taking me to an auto race when I was just a little boy — an AMAZING memory and something I wanted to do ever since but it only happened just that once. I would have happily gone every day !!

As a 3 year old, I made him proud while concurrently

amazing all the neighbors by correctly identifying any make of car, on sight, provided it was a car from the 1950's !! The hidden value of *Chilton's Auto Repair Manual* having photos of the grilles of cars, made manifest in real time. My relationship to cars was "complicated" because my relationship with my parents was complicated and cars and parents, in my family, are intimately linked. Irony, indeed, for someone who is perhaps the reincarnation of a famous racing driver in a prior lifetime.

the handsome man with Jet black hair and his little blonde son . . .
a complicated relationship; some very good things, some not so much
my father and me . . . sometime in the faraway land of the late 1950's

I also, as only a 3 or 4 year old could, *clashed* with my father and his friends by insisting that foreign cars were *better* than ones made in America . . . why drive some lame Plymouth or Pontiac when you could drive an Alfa Romeo or Maserati !!!! From where, exactly, did this *attitude* spring?

My dad was an auto mechanic who also worked as a tool and die maker in a Fisher Body plant for General Motors. He was an auto racing fan, too, and I remember watching the Indy 500 and other races on TV together. His favorite driver, a man upon whom Lady Luck never smiled at Indianapolis, was Lloyd Ruby.

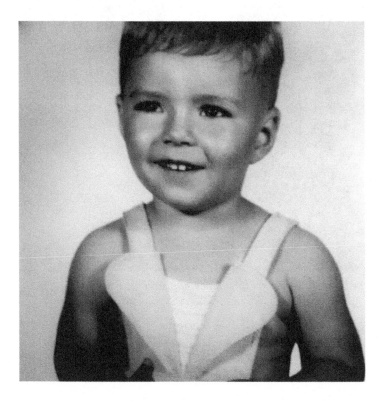

No doubt the parents I had — a father who turned me off of cars and a mother who did everything in her power to "slow me down" . . . were "pre-ordained" to keep me from following my "natural instincts" — perhaps so I would be ***obsessed*** with figuring out why I *saw the things* I did and what it all might mean.

****

As a baby my nickname was "Pep" (because I was so active) and the family story is that I was "injected with the Go-Go needle". This was meant to be funny but it was certainly not funny to me.

My mother was riddled with clinical anxiety, an endless stream of "nerve pills" always at the ready. An active daredevil child was the last thing she wanted and so, as time went on, the clamps on my movement became heavier and more pervasive.

An only child, I was, pretty much literally, drugged into submission through food and an endless tsunami of needless medication. Munchausen by Proxy, live and 3-D.

I wanted to GO; she wanted me to sit still . . . guess who won, at least short-term.

A tragedy . . . or a gift.

191

age 63, the reincarnation (perhaps) of a professional athlete?

It all depends, I guess, (like so many things in life) on how you *choose* to look at it and from what vantage point you're looking. I choose, NOW, to see it as a *gift*, a catalyst to help me find God and find some things, too, that are *important* in knowing how best to live in accordance with God and Spirit . . . ultimately a blessing, but this was a gift that came, initially, with a pretty hefty *price tag*.

The question one is likely to always ask in cases like this is "did the memories of racing cars and all that went with the ups downs and all arounds of Achille Varzi's life *show up* in my life, even as a little boy, as *predispositions* towards certain things or attitudes?"

Was there a little bit (or a whole lot) of reincarnated race car driver in the 3 year old identifying every car that came by? Did I feel something deep within me (coming from who knows where) as a little boy watching those cars run around an oval track, going faster and faster and sometimes crashing into one another? What does/can it all mean?

These are questions to which there are no easy answers.

****

As a little boy, I only wanted framed photos of antique cars on my bedroom wall. Nothing else. I also, (God, mysterious ways, that speech) lived in a town (Hamilton, Ohio) famous for its annual antique car parade, something to which I looked forward breathlessly every year.

Another "odd" kind of memory, as I think back on it, was my reaction to two films I used to see on our Black and White TV back in the early 1960's. One starred Clark Gable and the other one starred Kirk Douglas and Gilbert Roland.

Each was about racing and I remember being glued to the TV every time either of those films appeared — and they seemed to come on quite often, too. The Clark Gable movie was *To Please a Lady* (1950) and the other one, with Kirk Douglas, was *The Racers* (1955).

I *reacted* to those films !! Absolutely glued to whatever was happening. Of course, I gave zero fucks about any scenes with kissing or talking or wandering through the European countryside or whatever, but I had to stay close by just in case they jumped in a car and took off. Whenever they were *racing*, I was fully locked in to whatever was showing on our 25 inch b/w screen.

Why? Once again, a question with no easy answer.

****

Forty years of looking under Destiny's Fig Leaf and I am only marginally closer to understanding the root cause to my "car thing" as a preschooler than when I first started. But, there's *something* . . . not sure what but I do believe there's a *reason* (even if I can't fully understand it) behind this fascination with 1930's racing cars and Auto Union and Achille Varzi. I realize there are millions of little boys playing with cars and trucks who are car crazy but I still think all this means something, *specific* . . . to me that goes beyond the normal fascination with Tonka Toys or Matchbox Cars. Don't know what !! But something.

And I think whatever that something *is* . . . is important.

"When the green flag drops, the bullshit stops"
Jack Brabham

Twenty

Chequered Flag

Was I Achille Varzi, the Italian racing champion who derailed his career because of a fondness for blondes and morphine? Who knows. Do I look like him, in a crazy yes we're twins kind of way? Uh, yeah

This doesn't mean I was Achille Varzi and therein lies the root to my obsession (and, for far too long, *madness*)

Do I have memories of racing old cars in what seems to be the 1930's? Yes

But that doesn't mean these memories are real

And they could also be valid past life memories but "belong" to someone else

Translated: is it possible I simply picked Varzi because he fits and we look soooooooooo much alike, when (in truth) this is no different than me looking a little bit like John Davidson or Shaun Cassidy or Justin Bieber

I don't know and I'll *never* know. Sooooo, I spend hour upon hour *contemplating*

What it may mean and how it might work

There are no absolutes in my universe as both a psychic who "sees things" and predicts things

And as a past life researcher / "Akashic Reader"

I can offer no means of absolute validation

Are there black holes? Who knows but we construct a theory and on we go

Do I *believe* I am the reincarnation of Achille Varzi? Actually, I do

But I can never be sure, never prove it, never fully KNOW

****

so how, exactly, do I "find" these "past lives", come up with the idea I might have been, in this case, Achille Varzi, racing driver?

an interesting needle in a haystack kind of process, for sure . . . stories and images somehow just "come" to me, especially in relationship to PLACES or strings of events

the place itself always has a strong pull for me (what is called "karmic resonance") . . . certain locations just "light up"

I end up doing endless google searches, looking for certain "combinations" of elements . . . and since my peeps are obscure, always somehow leaving some small footnote in the history books — or I would certainly never find them (at least not searching like this !!)

they are not too easy to find !!

sometimes I get lucky and see something and the thing I see "lights up" and when it does I then look more deeply into that particular pile

once I find a potential match, then I look at the photos . . . does this person look like me; because if they don't, I reject them

and, if the stories have all the bizarre bits and pieces and the face goes together, then I have to find their birth date and do an astrology matching

I haven't talked about Astrology in this book, but it is a *critical* piece for me in validating a match, to the extent that any potential match *can* be validated . . . don't be surprised if you see another book by me some day looking at "Astrology and Past Lives"

all these disparate elements must come together *first* — as they did with Achille Varzi (there are others, too — but I'm saving *those* stories for later), but he *showed up* only after a long long very long and quite *frustrating* attempt to find him

And thus the wheels on the Bugatti go round (once more)

****

here we are, at the end of *all* the searching, with Achille Varzi, my (theoretical) past life . . . a famous (at the time) Grand Prix driver from Italy, briefly the highest paid athlete in the world

who stole his team mate's wife, a sleek Germanic blonde who turned him onto morphine and well, as most of us could easily imagine, morphine addiction and super fast cars are not typically seen as good bed fellows

and so the highest paid athlete in the world destroyed his career and there you go (just as I have often done myself; sex and love are intoxicating brews, don't you know) . . . as I've pointed out earlier, there are many elements of Varzi's personality that seem to vibe with me, in many different ways

elegant, slightly aloof, VERY quick hands and feet, highly competitive, both über-focused and yet, somehow, easily distracted, *seemingly* ruthless (up to a point) when he wanted *to achieve* something, analytical yet dreamy, too, a magnet for women (for a time, anyway) and *uncompromising* . . . and stubborn, can't forget stubborn

and, of course, highly emotional and occasionally self-destructive even as he forged a career in which he was seen as cool calm and collected in an arena in which most were not

****

Varzi was a champion, competing year in, year out and then, suddenly, he was gone. Kicked out of the sport in which he excelled. Driven (#irony) to win, he was still graceful in defeat; as a motorcycle racer he won an award for sportsmanship when he crashed his motorbike into a wall rather than hit a fallen racer

He was full-on *rock star*, rich, glamorous, *dangerous*, knighted in 1931 by the Italian king, a new girl in every town, photographers and journalists tracking his every move and then, pretty much overnight, "he wasn't"

His winnings, not including appearance fees or any other streams of income, for 1934 alone would be equivalent to over $1.2 Million today. Literally the highest paid athlete in the world (in any sport), within just 3 years he was addicted to morphine and unable to race, in part because other drivers considered him erratic and potentially dangerous to them!

Shunned by many "in society" after this rapid "fall from grace", his was, without doubt, an up and down existence. This pattern is not unlike my own and these types of life rhythms, *styles of engagement*, in my opinion (and theory) tend to carry over from one lifetime to the next. Varzi and I *both* seem most comfortable when going one of just two speeds: FAST and PARK

The *real story* of Achille Varzi, his legacy as one of the most talented drivers of all time, has been buried . . . ignominy, shame, a "cone of silence". In *The Greatest Racing Driver: The Life and Times of Great Drivers, with a Logical Analysis Revealing the Greatest,* author Angus Dougall says of Varzi's life that it was "like a melodramatic tragedy, but with no explanations"

As to Varzi's talent, he sums it up with this statement: "He really was that good"

Dougall also writes that "It seems strange that this interesting man with the talent to run with Nuvolari, Fagioli, Carraciola, and Rosemeyer, and sometimes beat them, has not been covered more extensively than he has. Maybe he was just too much of an enigma"

Author Di Giorgio Terruzzi says of Varzi: "how come a great driver capable of winning a lot and everywhere, of really rivaling Nuvolari — his double — has been forgotten, remained in a cone of shadow? To find answers, it was a question of reconstructing — amidst the obstinate silence of those who had known him — a long tragic journey"

Oliver Harry wrote a wonderful piece for *Carboretta* entitled *Why You Should Know About: Achille Varzi*. He states: "The most fascinating of stories tend to follow a roughly similar arc. It reads as follows: the main protagonist rises through the ranks, tasting the spoils of victory along the way — only to suffer a dramatic fall. Undeterred, they pick themselves out of the dust and reclaim their throne, but with ultimately tragic consequences. It is a wholly Shakespearean template, but one that Varzi emulated spectacularly during his colourful life"

Harry later writes "his downfall was as dramatic and erratic as any in world sport. A serial race winner in the early 1930s, by the end of the decade Varzi was holed up in a Milanese hotel room clinging to a morphine addiction"

There are dozens of stories just like the ones I've shared. All pointed to the Shakepearean rise and fall of a great talent and the subsequent white out of his career and accomplishments

Many of the lies most often repeated about Varzi's life come from *Speed was my Life*, by Alfred Neubauer, the racing manager of the Mercedes-Benz Grand Prix team from 1926 to 1955. I truly can't even stand to look at the man's photo . . . literally. Pretty good chance that many of the stories in his memoir are distortions if not outright fabrications

In a profile about him at www.uniquecarsandparts.com.au, the author said of Varzi: "Many who saw him at his best consider that, for sheer artistry at the wheel, he will never have an equal. He made the art of Grand Prix driving seem absurdly simple, as is the case with perfectionists in any activity. He could have been the greatest the world has ever known"

. . . the *greatest* the world has ever known

Hated by the Fascists, no doubt not on the Master Race Preferred Guest List with the Nazis, either and scorned by many of his fellow drivers (either due to his personality "rubbing them the wrong way" or, perhaps, jealousy at his seemingly *effortless* ability to win so many races), he truly was an OUTLAW in Motor Sports

Achille Varzi (center) on the podium after winning The Tunis Grand Prix, 1931

All this was made even worse after his very public affair with Ilse Pietsch and his rapid descent into addiction . . . leading to, literal, revocation of his license and banishment from the sport; the *true* story of Varzi's life and career will likely never be known

There are lots of dark holes into which one might jump in attempting to unravel the "enigma" of Achille Varzi. However, this isn't a book about Varzi's life — it's, instead, a look back at how I went searching for some kind of answer to the question "is it possible I lived before?"

. . . nor is this a book making claim that I *was* Achille Varzi, although I *believe it* quite strongly for myself yet I am also rational enough (professional psychic, and the *baggage* that comes with that, or not) to realize nothing I say will ever be enough to build a definitive case, yes/no, one way or another. Some will look at the photos, read my words, and think "dude, that (for sure) is YOU !!"

Others will find a multiplicity of holes in my presentation and say "not convincing" (or worse). I present my story and my ideas in the hopes that my search for some kind of *answer* will shed some light on what's possible as well as what's *necessary* for those of us who hear this past life dog whistle. Are we all crazee ?? No one knows; certainly not me and I cannot give definitive proof that will convince those unwilling, or unable, to be convinced

Some people believe those who die violent deaths come back quickly. Perhaps too quickly. Others believe those whose legacy has been tarnished, unfairly, return to "clear their name". Is that why a famous racing driver, killed doing what he loved, subject to gossip and lies after his death by those who stood to gain most by "distorting the truth" chose to return in the body of a young man *obsessed* with finding out if reincarnation is real and obsessed, too, with understanding why he kept "seeing things"?

Who knows. Maybe

But also "maybe not"

I believe reincarnation is real. I believe in God and I believe God and Love are synonyms. But these are my *opinions* and I am still searching for answers about how to live, and die, most effectively

I want to leave you with a few quotations about Mr. Varzi from those who knew him. Perhaps their words will offer some clues as to the man's character and perhaps, as well, their words may offer some modest reflection on my own

****

The great Juan Manuel Fangio, 5 time World Drivers' Champion, said of Varzi and his legacy: *"Varzi was, to me, a god. He spoke with great simplicity, and gave me precious advice. He is probably the driver I have most admired in my life, a man who cared only for his art"*

To honor Varzi's influence, when Fangio came to Europe and started racing in Formula 1 he called his team *Scuderia Achille Varzi*

Enzo Ferrari said of him: *"This racing driver was a real man: intelligent, calculating, aggressive when necessary, quick to take advantage of the first weakness, the first error, the first problem for the opponent. I would say ruthless and not easy to understand ... stubborn as few people are ... "*

The following epitaph was delivered in 1948 at Varzi's funeral in Galliate, Italy. Attended by over 15,000 mourners, his body lay in state, watched over in a constant vigil by his friends, for three days and nights on the chassis of a race car in the church at Galliate

All the greatest drivers of Europe, except for his dear friend and rival, Tazio Nuvolari, who was ill and would, himself, die of a lung disease only five years later, in 1953, were there to pay tribute to his life and legacy. It goes like this:

****

"Perhaps you were destined to die, Achille, because in your driving there was something of that genius which is one of Nature's greatest mysteries, and Nature strives to destroy those who come too close to her.

"Beethoven was struck with deafness when he seemed about to transcend man's powers of musical expression. Galileo was blinded when he tried to probe infinity and its laws. Leonardo da Vinci's hands were crippled when he was about to come nearer to perfection than any man before him.

"And you too, Achille, were destroyed when you sought to cross the known frontiers of man-made speed. Now you are preparing for another race, the last great race. A race without danger, without care or sorrow..."

Live FAST . . . Achille Varzi on his way to victory at The Grand Prix of Monaco, 1933

Further Reading

For additional background detailing the complex relationship between sport and the Nazis in the 1930's, you may want to check out *Racing the Silver Arrows: Mercedes Benz versus Auto Union, 1934-1939* (1986) and *Auto Union Album, 1934-1939* (1998) both by Chris Nixon, *Hitler's Motor Racing Battles: The Silver Arrows under the Swastika* by Eberhard Reuss, translated by Angus McGeoch (2006), *How Hitler Hijacked World Sport: The World Cup, the Olympics, the Heavyweight Championship and Grand Prix* by Christopher Hilton (2011) and *Driving Forces: The Grand Prix Racing World Caught in the Maelstrom of the Third Reich* by Peter Stevenson (2000).

Two very interesting fictional accounts of racing in the 1930's with Achille Varzi as one of the primary characters are *The Last Great Race* by Mark Morey (2016) and *Tracks: Racing the Sun* by Sandro Martini (2014).

An Italian film, *When Nuvolari Runs: The Flying Mantuan* (2018) — a film I have tried to track down by cannot, although I've seen clips, deals with the relationship between Varzi and his rival, and friend, Tazio Nuvolari and it has come to my attention, too, that Italian playwright Edoardo Erba wrote a play about Varzi's life entitled *Blind Curve*.

From Erba's website, he offers this description of his play: *Four acts. Seven characters. Drama. The dramatic story of love and drugs of Achille Varzi, the Formula One driver and historic rival of Tazio Nuvolari.*

Another valuable resource on Varzi's racing career is *Bugatti: A Racing History* by David Venables (2002). Venables says this about Varzi: "In the early 1930's, Varzi was probably the best driver of his era, Nuvolari was still approaching his peak and probably only Chiron was in the same class at that time. A quiet, elegant, and introverted man, Varzi was perhaps the most talented driver ever to race a Bugatti."

****

Turning to reincarnation, I have read lots and lots of books over the past 40 years about this fascinating topic. One book that has been essential to my understanding of reincarnation is, in fact, an Astrology book: *Astrology, Karma & Transformation: The Inner Dimensions of the Birth Chart* (1978) by astrologer Stephen Arroyo.

Many of the best books you'll find on the subject, in my opinion, are old paperbacks from the 1960's and 1970's. There are numerous fine introductions to this topic available as well as several quite fascinating personal narratives of people trying to discover (as I've attempted) their *own* past lives.

One book I particularly enjoyed was *The Boy Who Knew Too Much: An Astounding True Story of a Young Boy's Past-Life Memories* by Cathy Byrd, detailing her son (and baseball prodigy) Christian Haupt's possible past life as Yankee great Lou Gehrig and Christian's memories as a two and three year old of being a "tall baseball player".

Other important books (and this is just skimming the surface) about searching for past lives include *Looking for Carroll Beckwith: The True Stories of a Detective's Search for his Past Life* (1999) by Robert L. Snow, *Someone Else's Yesterday: The Confederate General and Connecticut Yankee: A Past Life Revealed (2003)* by Jeffrey J. Keene . . . *Soul Survivor: The Reincarnation of a World War II Fighter Pilot (2010)* by Bruce and Andrea Leininger, with Ken Gross . . . *Marilyn Monroe Returns: The Healing of a Soul* (2006) by Dr. Adrian Finkelstein and *By Love Reclaimed: Jean Harlow Returns to Clear Her Husband's Name* (2012) by Dr. Adrian Finkelstein and Valerie Franich . . . as well as going totally "old school" — *The Search for Bridey Murphy* (1956) by Morie Bernstein.

****

I mentioned Dr. Ian Stevenson's work earlier, as well as Dr. Adrian Finkelstein and Dr. Paul Von Ward. Dr. Jim Tucker has continued the work of Dr. Stevenson at the University of Virginia and his research into children and past life memories is incredibly valuable. Dr. Walter Semkiw has compiled an amazing body of work over the years and for people seeking more information about reincarnation, Walter's books and website are a good place to start.

A wonderful treasure trove for people seeking information about a host of spiritual topics (including reincarnation), and one that people don't seem to talk about much anymore — although I think they should, are the books of actress Shirley MacLaine. I think her books are incredible and well worth seeking out. To me, her books (and ideas) never "go out of style". Same, too, with every book ever written by Sanaya Roman !!

I also want to give a shout out to my good friends Brian Hunter and Tara Sutphen and recommend their books, especially *The Hunter Equation* (2018) by Brian and *Blame it on Your Past Lives: Personal Problems and Supernatural Solutions* (1993) by Tara, as magical resources (from two VERY magical people) on reincarnation and spirituality as well as Steven Forrest's excellent *Yesterday's Sky: Astrology and Reincarnation* (2008).

****

One past life "match" that has never been treated in a book, in part because the young man died tragically at a young age (twice !!), is the story of Carl Edon, who may have (in a prior lifetime) been a Luftwaffe pilot for Germany who died in World War II . Carl was born in England, quite close to where this particular German pilot died when his plane was shot down thirty years earlier.

Of all the stories I've seen about reincarnation, Carl Edon *clangs me* most. There's even more to this story than I've mentioned here . . . If you aren't familiar with this case, do yourself a favor and google his name. VERY COMPELLING.

****

There, sadly, aren't many full length biographies of Achille Varzi, in part because there are so many gaps in his story with few documented sources upon which to look to fill them. Author Giorgio Terruzzi is probably the most knowledgeable biographer today of Varzi's life and career. He penned, in 1991, a bio of Varzi entitled *Una curva cieca - Vita di Achille Varzi*. However, there just aren't a lot of bios that go into much depth about this amazing man's equally amazing life and many of the stories about him, in my opinion, are mythology, not *objective* truth.

Achille Varzi is buried in his hometown of Galliate, Italy where you can also find The Achille Varzi Museum, located in the Castello Visconteo Sforzesco. It is possible to arrange tours of the Castle, which also includes a visit to the "Achille Varzi the lord of the steering wheel" Museum Hall located in the south wing. You can also, each year, celebrate *Achille Varzi Day* in Galliate, held every Summer.

Next Steps

⟋⟍⟋⟍

This book was complete. All I needed to do was upload it to *Amazon* and it would be birthed into the world. I planned to do it right after Thanksgiving but woke up Thanksgiving morning and saw an email from *Hulu*, offering me a membership for $1.99 a month, which I decided to do.

This morning, the day after Thanksgiving, I did a search, "reincarnation", and watched an episode of *Ancient Aliens*, entitled *The Replicants*. Most of the shows I watch about reincarnation are kind of boring to me now, although once upon a time they most assuredly were not. But this episode, *The Replicants*, I thought was very well done and kind of *clanged me*, which is Andyspeak for "resonated with me".

Another show that clanged me was on TV a few years back, *The Ghost Inside My Child*. Some of the stories seemed iffy to me but one that hit me hard was the story of Amy Pierce and her possible past life as child star Lucille Ricksen. I was very intrigued by this particular story and sought out Amy and her mother Theresa and invited them on my (then) radio show in 2014. I feel quite strongly that Amy's story is "the truth" and there are many more stories of young children with past life memories that are simply incredible.

I had these types of memories as a young boy, too, but they're long since gone now.

Adults seeking out past life memories and trying to reconstruct past life timelines face many difficulties. Is regression the answer? Can spontaneous recollections "be trusted"? Who, really, can say?

****

Past life regressions changed my life. This is literally true and not declared with a false sense of hyperbole. My class on past life regressions in San Francisco in July, 1979 opened up an entirely new way of seeing myself and seeing life, in general. But, over time, I grew to distrust past life regressions as vehicles for "confirming" past life memories.

To me, there has to be more — a consistent *something* that you can see and say "there it *is*" . . . and I began constructing models, many of which (over the years) I threw out, of what actually "might reincarnate" and began looking for *that thing* first and worrying less about specific "past life" memories.

I took a class with Dr. A. M. Krasner, developer of "The Krasner Method of Clinical Hypnotherapy", in 1991 as a prerequisite to certification in clinical hypnotherapy. I have been regressed and have regressed others literally hundreds of times. There is a tremendous value in past life regressions and, no doubt, sometimes they work and open a window into a person's past life.

But not all regressions, in my opinion, lead to "valid memories" and so, just for myself, I began to pay less and less attention to work that focused on memories retrieved under hypnosis as "proof of reincarnation" and more and more to work that suggested there were visible biological markers indicative of some form of past life *continuity*.

Everyone has an opinion and this is mine. Again, with all things that deal with reincarnation, NO ONE KNOWS. But we construct our theories, devise our tests and see what happens. If the results of the test are encouraging, then we move forward drilling down deeper and deeper, seeking additional levels of clarity. This is what I've done for over 40 years and will keep doing as long as I am able to do so.

****

One of the panelists on *The Replicants* was Bob Good, author of *The Science of Reincarnation* (2012). I have watched some of his videos on *youtube* and read his book and think his work is incredibly well thought out and also of great value as we move forward in our attempts to "map the territory".

Another body of work mentioned in *The Replicants* are theories presented by Emeritus Professor of Mathematics at Oxford University, Roger Penrose, and Dr. Stuart Hameroff on quantum consciousness and microtubules. I am not a physicist nor a brain researcher, but in my limited understanding of their theory, it appears that we share similar ideas as to how "consciousness works".

Physicist David Bohm and biologist Rupert Sheldrake come quickly to mind as people who have presented ideas that I realize, after the fact, are similar to ones I developed, after they did and on a much more limited scale, on my own.

Of course, there are many other scientists offering incredible insights into "how the world works" but I do not have a solid grounding in physics and mathematics and have only a layman's understanding of (and familiarity with) the work currently outstanding.

Physicists are the mystics now. And mysticism and physics speak, in quite remarkable ways, the same language more often than you might suspect.

****

I didn't have physics or religion to tell me what was real. Everywhere I looked, I came up empty. Nothing seemed to satisfy my need to know "who I was" or "where I came from" so (as I result) I was forced to go out totally on my own looking for answers about life and how "it all worked" because, truthfully, I couldn't figure out how to live with the answers I had. They didn't make sense to me and I wasn't willing to accept something just because others said so.

Hand-me-down tales from people repeating hand-me-down tales that had been recycled and repeated with no thought whatsoever . . . that was how it seemed to me. People thought they had an answer but what they knew they knew only because they'd been told that the person telling them "knew". Far as I could tell, there was no other reason. But they didn't know . . . and most people just didn't seem to care, so long as they only said what was *acceptable*.

That, for sure, ain't me.

I wouldn't (or couldn't) accept *any* story without first examining it for myself and, upon reflection, and analysis, and listening to my own "inner voice", ultimately I rejected the hand-me-down tales everyone else kept spinning.

****

Reincarnation is *the truth* . . . God is the truth. There is a spiritual world, just as there is a physical world you can see and touch, so, too, can you see and touch with your inner eye the world of the Spirit, if you only try and can, first, tune out those telling you not to.

I may have been Achille Varzi, I may not have been. It's impossible to say. But I feel 10,000% confident in saying I was someone, somewhere, before I got here "this time".

And, so, too . . . were YOU !!

I feel equally confident in saying we're not an accident. We come from a world of Spirit and we have a divine purpose in coming here, as many times *as we may choose*.

Take a moment, or two, or fifty thousand and examine things for yourself. Trust your instincts, hear you *own* voice, find the magical creature within you, waiting to reveal itself to you, whenever you're finally ready. God is within you and so, too, are you within God.

There's a **reason** you're here.

"A little while, a moment of rest upon the wind, and another woman shall bear me."
~ Khalil Gibran

L-O-V-E

About the Author

Andrew Brewer, *The Rock 'n Roll Psychic*, is an internationally televised clairvoyant, astrologer, and akashic reader, listed in over 30 publications as "One of the Top 50 Psychics in the World", "One of the Top 100 Lightworkers in the World", and "One of the Top 30 Psychics in the United States".

Andrew was chosen as "The Man of the Year" and "The Male Lightworker of the Year" for 2016 and 2017 in polling conducted by *Times Square Press New York* and *Revue Voyance & Parapsychologie* from a list of over 17,000 candidates from 85 countries.

Selected for membership in the "Lightworkers World Hall of Fame", Andrew has been listed as the:

#2 Best Male Psychic in the United States

#2 Best Male Medium in the United States

#3 Best Metaphysical Teacher in the United States

#5 Top Lightworker / Practitioner of Divinatory Arts in the World

About the Author

Andrew was the featured clairvoyant on *Kebrina's Psychic Answer*, which aired in both the United States and Canada from 1992-94 and has been profiled in articles in *USA Today*, *The Los Angeles Times*, and *The Columbus Dispatch*.

Author 8 books and creator of 3 Tarot/Divination Decks, Andrew is a former corporate executive as well as a film actor in Hollywood. He is also a Certified Professional Boxing Fitness Trainer and seen as a world recognized authority on reincarnation and past lives.

A client once labeled him "Human Xanax" and he likes to think of himself as a cool head in times of crisis and hopefully a good, kind person, overall.

For more info please go to www.andrew-brewer.com or www.karmicoutlaw.com

Made in the USA
Monee, IL
14 October 2022

15847317R00135